22 FEB. 21

D1484943

Bricks, Mortar and Other People's Money

By Liam Ryan

Cover design by Studio02. Additional graphics created by Freepik.

Dedications

Hollie Ryan, my wife - always supporting me and taking me from one place to another.

Acknowledgments

Jay Munoz my business partner, Jessen James, James Nicholson, Dave our first investor and all other investors. Also a word of thanks to Paul Ryan and Mica Parmar.

Contents

About the author

Liam has been a businessman right from the word go. From being a hustler in the school playground he went on to become an international entrepreneur heading up a number of multi-million pound companies. If you want to spend time in his company these days a one-to-one mentor session will cost you £5,000.

Alongside his business partner Jay Munoz he co-founded Assets For Life three years ago and as a testament to his property freedom formula Assets For Life has enjoyed rapid growth.

Back in 2014 their portfolio had a nil valuation. Cut to today and the portfolio value has just reached a staggering 12.6 million. It is the secret to this rapid growth that Liam wants to share so that you too can enjoy phenomenal success.

Introduction

Start getting excited right now.

Why?

Because this book will change your life.

I know that is a big claim but I am a man of my word and I never say anything I don't mean.

My Name is Liam Ryan and I am one of the co-founders of Assets For Life. Over the last couple of years we have been able to raise over £4m in joint venture finance. On top of that we have been able to add over £12m worth of property to our portfolio and most of that being done via joint venture finance. And when we talk about raising joint venture finance, we're going to be talking about 'no money down' deals.

In simple terms we buy houses using other people's money.

I promise that if you want to create huge personal wealth and create your own property portfolio with no financial risk to you whatsoever, the secrets revealed in this book will ensure that you do so.

This book contains a unique and proven formula that is guaranteed to create a multimillion pound property portfolio using none of your own money and if you follow the simple six step guide your future as a property millionaire is assured.

This is not hot air - it's fact.

Right now there are people out there who are inches away from becoming property millionaires and you will be hearing from a host of our mentees who have achieved real success beyond there wildest dreams by using the six step no money down blueprint system.

Can it really be that simple? You read a book and become a property millionaire. Well, yes... and no. You have to do the work, you have to follow the process and you have to really want it.

If you are up for that then read on.

They say a journey of a thousand miles starts with one single step. Well, I invite you now to make the first six steps of your journey to a new life. Let your adventure begin!

Chapter One

What is your 'why'?

Now, one of the biggest questions that I get asked all of the time is "Liam, how can I go and build a multimillion pound property portfolio using none of my own money? I can see that what you have done at Assets fort Life has been absolutely amazing in just the last couple of years but I just can't see myself doing it."

My response is quite simple:

'How' is easy.

How to do it is set.

The question I ask them and the question I want you to consider right now is, 'why?'

Why do you want to do it?

What is your current situation and why do you want it to change?

Where are you now?

Let me give you a few different scenarios and see if any of them chime with you:

Perhaps you're in a position at the moment where there's never enough money left at the end of the month. It might be that you, like so many others in our country and all around the world are in some bad debt. Believe me, I've been there. I know that feeling. You're getting up every day from a sleepless, worry-filled night and it just feels like you've got this massive sack of problems on your back that you just don't know how to shake off.

Or:

Perhaps you've been in property for some time and you've now run out of cash. Maybe your money is tied up in an existing property portfolio, perhaps you've used all of your savings, and maybe your property journey has become stagnant.

You know you want to do something bigger and better, but you just don't know how to go about finding the funds in order to carry on with your property journey.

Or:

It might be that you are currently in a position where you are a wage slave, simply exchanging your time for money. Yes, the bills are being paid but there is no excitement any more and the spring in your step has long since gone.

Maybe you are just going through the grind, feeling more and more frustrated as every uneventful day passes without change or challenge. This is something that happens to many people at one point or another in their lives and careers.

You just wake up one morning to discover the spark and spirit of adventure that you once had many years ago has disappeared. Somehow the pressures and demands that everyday life thrusts upon you has all but completely extinguished that fire in your belly that used to keep you moving forward with excitement and verve.

Or:

You might be in a corporate job where you're working so hard for so much of the time that you've lost sight of the reason you're doing it in the first place. You might be working so many hours that you don't have time with your friends and you're not able to spend quality time with your family.

Or:

You might simply want to have more time and more freedom. Freedom to do what you want to do and choose when you want to do it - more freedom to make your own choices, to go where you want, and to start living the life of you've always dreamed of. The life that you desire and the life you deserve.

Or:

Maybe you're getting to a point where you're reaching retirement and you know you're not going to have enough funds to give you the lifestyle that you want.

Do any of the above situations match your own?

Of course, I don't know about you or where you're currently at the moment, but how does this sound?

Building a multimillion pound property portfolio using none of your own money

Creating a dynamic and exciting new career

Creating greater self confidence
Having the lifestyle of your dreams
Spending more time with your family
Spending more time with your friends
More parties
More fun
More money

I want to tell you right here, right now that by reading this book and following the exact system that I'm going to be sharing with you, all this can be yours. Like I said before:

We know HOW you can do it

But

You need to know WHY you want to do it.

There is an incredible book called 'Think and Grow Rich'. If you haven't read it I suggest you do. It is the absolute blueprint for every business and success book ever written.

The author, Napoleon Hill had this to say about your WHY:

'There is one quality that you must posses to win, and that is definiteness of purpose, the knowledge of what you want and a burning desire to achieve it'.

What is your definiteness of purpose? What is your WHY?

To help you gain a better idea of what your WHY is I want you to get a pen and paper because we are going to do something called...

Think on paper

Did you know that if you have your dreams, goals and aspirations written down you are ten times more likely to achieve them? When you write down your goal you are taking it from the intellectual place in your head into the real world. You are crystalising the ideas and turning them into a physical reality. It suddenly actually exists for you to see and feel (even if it is only on a sheet of A4). Suddenly the mere act of writing down your goal gives it a real world energy that will stimulate you to action.

Do this exercise right now:

I want you to imagine where you want to be in two years and write down ten amazing things about your achievements and acquisitions i.e. what you've done and what material things you've got.

For example, where are you living in two years' time?

Where do you take your holidays?

How many holidays do you have each year?

How much money do you have in the bank etc?

I want you to think big, go outside what you currently see as possible, aim for the stars. Think about your business, your lifestyle, your portfolio.

Now write down ten reasons WHY you want to build your property portfolio.

Take a little time to do this and when you've done it I want you to read the list and feel the sense of excitement it gives you that you are going to make this list a reality.

When you have finished and taken time to read through your list of ten amazing goals you can carry on with the book.

Stop reading and do this now!

All done? Good.

Welcome back.

The first time I ever did the exercise you have just gone through I ended up somehow losing the list. Amazingly, about a year or so later, I stumbled across it and guess what? I had achieved eight out of the ten things on my list. And you know what? It happened effortlessly!

By setting out my WHY I had something to aim for. The rewards were clearly signposted for me and as a result I knew how to orient myself towards achieving them. It works like magic.

Another thing you can do is to create a vision board with pictures and images of your goals and aspirations. Once you've done it hang it on the wall over your office desk. This is a hugely powerful way of continually feeding your mind with WHY you are creating your own portfolio.

Not to get to deep into the psychological reasons why this works, all you need to know is that once you know what you're aiming for your mind has a target but without a target in the first place you can't aim at anything.

So...where are you now?

At the beginning of this chapter you didn't know what you were aiming for. Now you do!

Pretty soon you can start doing no money down deals and take the first steps to creating your multi-million pound property portfolio. As a result of doing that, your life will be transformed and you will go into what I call 'the fourth dimension'.

When people ask me what I mean by the fourth dimension I simply tell them 'heaven on earth'.

The fourth dimension is living in a world where you have total peace of mind and everything you want. A place where you make all the decisions, where there is no pressure, where there is only excitement, achievement and where you are surrounded by the rewards of all your hard work.

Sound like heaven to you?

The fourth dimension is only six steps away.

Chapter Two

Why listen to me?

Now, it might be that you and I have met at one of the many amazing Assets For Life seminars that we continually run up and down the country, in which case, you already have a good feeling that I'm a straight up guy.

However, if you have plucked this book from the shelf of your local WHSmiths you might want a little bit of background on me. Check if I've got any previous and all that (I haven't by the way)!

Here we go then, a little bit about me. Hopefully by the end of this chapter you will have the feeling that I am a straight up guy too.

So like I said earlier, my name is Liam Ryan and I'm one of the co-founders of Assets For Life.

I created Assets For Life back in 2015 alongside my wonderful, amazing business partner Jay Munoz. Actually, I can't talk about me and not talk about Jay. So maybe this chapter should really be called:

Me, Jay and how we created Assets For Life.

So how I did go and meet Jay? Well that story starts a very long time ago.

I'm a serial entrepreneur and venture capitalist. I'd lived abroad for 14 years setting up various businesses and selling them on once they had reached pinnacle performance. I had enjoyed the experience and travelled the world with my businesses but after so much time away from England I got to the stage where I wanted to come back home.

I moved back to the UK about five years ago and guess what I did? That's right, I set up a new business straightaway. No sooner had my plane hit the tarmac than I was drawing up plans for a business in the new sector of growth, renewable energy.

I was starting to think about the environment and my kids' future, I wanted to do something that would help to make a positive impact while satisfying my entrepreneurs itch! Plus the government had been running a fantastic incentive to encourage people to buy solar paneling that meant everyone was a winner. People were getting a government grant to buy the panels and then getting free energy for life. And who was going to sell them the panels? Me! Perfect, a win-win situation for everybody. Just what I like.

So after a great deal of time setting up, doing due diligence, market research, sourcing office space and initial recruitment the doors finally opened in 2014.

We had a gala opening with a ribbon cutting ceremony all of our new staff members, Champagne, balloons streamers, press coverage, the lot.

It was a very special time, and I was feeling really proud of what I had achieved, a brand new company, employing 30 local people that was going to be good for the planet!

And it was a success! A huge success!

The business grew rapidly, and before I knew it we were up to 95 staff members, we were taking order after order of our lead product and I was in the throws of relocating our offices to accommodate even further growth.

I was living in the fourth dimension. Everything in my life was running like clockwork. I made all the decisions, my stress levels had all but disappeared and one morning I decided not to go into the office. That's fourth dimension living for you. Yes, on this day I was going to do something for me. On this day the office could run itself for a while. I decided to go to the gym. Little did I know that while I was working out a very big decision had been taken by a government minister, a policy shift that would have far-reaching and immediate consequences.

My workout had been brilliant. As I stood in the shower afterwards I actually remember singing 'Oh What A Beautiful Morning'. Little did I now what was about to happen and what a poor choice of song that was going to prove to be.

I remember walking into my office, protein shake in hand, feeling really pumped up for the day. But the second I walked through the door I knew something was wrong. I could just feel it. There was an eerie tension in the air.

All my key staff members were looking rather sheepish. Normally when I arrived people were all smiles but on this day no one was willing to look me in the eye. I went up to Donna my PA, 'What's going on?' I said. For a moment she just looked at me and then she said "Have you seen the latest news," and I said "I've not seen anything this morning, tell me what's going on." I could see all the staff were sneaking furtive glances at us. Donna ushered me silently into the boardroom and closed the door behind us with a gentle click.

We sat down on my black leather chairs with my white long boardroom desk, by this time my heart was beating like a drum. 'For God sakes Donna just spit it out will you', I barked, trying as hard as I could not to let the tension show in my voice.

'Liam' she said, 'the government have just announced that they're going to be cutting the feeding tariff for solar panels. Which means no more government funding for anyone buying their solar panels from us'.

Now, I don't know if you can relate to this, but in that moment, and it was just a split second, I experienced an eternity. The fourth dimension vanished in an instant. Everything was gone. I knew that my business was completely and utterly finished. It wasn't scalable, it wasn't sustainable, and I knew there and then that over the next few days I was going to have to run that business down to its absolute bare bones..

It was a gut-wrenching and terrifying shock. I felt terrible for all 95 of my staff members but I had no choice. I kept my 10 best people and said 85 painful, goodbyes to all those I was having to let go. Everyone was devastated and I, as a business owner, was practically destroyed.

That night and for many nights to follow I couldn't sleep a wink. I just couldn't get to sleep through the worry and gut wrenching anxiety of what was happening. I also knew that there was more pain to follow. I can tell you, I certainly shed a few tears.

A week later, I finally plucked up the courage to go and see my accountants. The final reckoning was yet to come.

My accountants were Dave and John in Billericay, good blokes with bad news, but I had to face up to the reality of what was going on so I jumped in my car, I drive down to their office.

As I arrived I remember there being this very distinct musky smell; they absolutely loved drinking coffee, and it was like gone off coffee smell an aroma I now always associate with fear. I sat down in their chair and I looked them in the eye and I said "what's the damage".

David looked at me, swallowed hard. He spoke very slowly and very quietly. "I'm very sorry to tell you this Liam," he said, "but you've lost £392,000."

£392,000!

Lost! Gone! Forever!

I wanted the ground to eat me up. All I can remember thinking to myself in that moment was 'if you don't change, nothing will change, if you don't change, nothing will change'.

I was gutted, but what could I do but bite the bullet and get back on the horse. Sitting around focusing on the calamity would solve nothing. It was a horrible week that followed but I kept my eyes facing forward, kept my team of ten close to me and vowed to solider on. We were still just about able to trade so I turned my attention to trying to create whatever sales I could.

About a week later, we're all sitting in silence in my office when the phone rings. One of my admin assistance picked it up and this voice on the other end of the line said, "Hello, I'm Jay Munoz. Look, I've heard the news, you guys have been calling me for quite some time. I'm now ready to have solar installed."

So my assistant booked the appointment, I jumped into my car, shot down to Colchester and met with Jay. True to his word he bought some solar panels and then he started to explain about him being a property investor. The conversation grew and as he spoke I realised that we had a great deal in common and his ideas were full of potential. We soon started to formulate a business model and the rest as they say is history.

As well as being a property investor Jay is also a chartered civil engineer. I'm so grateful to have found a partner who has so many strengths. He's a very intelligent guy who gets excited by a spreadsheet, has a love of numbers and an eye for property.

When I met Jay back in those dark days of 2015 I knew immediately that there was a synergy and I had this gut feeling that we could create something very, very special together. Deep down inside I could feel the faintest glimmer of the light at the end of the tunnel.

I was immediately struck by the warmth of his personality, his clarity and his business acumen. His credentials were highly impressive too, having worked on some of the biggest builds in the UK as a top project manager for Skanska and ISG, and he's worked on Heron Tower and The Walbrook.

But were we going to make a good fit as partners? After all it's a big decision.

This next piece of advice is worth a million pounds in itself:

When you get a business partner it's really important to make sure that you've got opposing skill sets.

There is no point in both of you being good at the same things.

As I just said, Jay loves a good spreadsheet! He really gets off on it. Not me! After about two or three minutes of staring at Microsoft Excel I feel seasick.

But Jay and I have a partnership of equals. So what do I bring to the table? I am more the public face of the company. I get up and do the bulk of any presentations that need doing, I manage and run the hugely successful Facebook page that yields so very much in the way of connections, awareness and client base. I'm more client facing. Jay has all the finance and logistics covered off to a T.

As individuals we simply could not have achieved the rapid success of Assets For Life. It would not have happened. Individually we both have a broad set of skills but together our talents strengths and abilities combine to create a partnership of extreme versatility and power.

Having spoken about the power of our differences I want to spend a moment to discuss the power of our similarities. Our alignments. Where we match in our intellectual placement.

In any business partnership it is vital that you both make sure that you are agreed on your vision and your values. Your vision and values must be shared and aligned.

Also you have to feel that there is an emotional connection between you where you can ultimately help each other, rely on each other and make tough decisions together. That way you give your best the best possible start to grow an amazing business. Just as we have done.

So remember, when the door closes, another door will open and what is really important is that when you see an opportunity you grab that opportunity with both hands. In that moment say 'yes'.

I had a decision to make - I could continue to feel sorry for myself or, as an entrepreneur, as a go-getter, as an action-taker make the decision to pick myself up, say yes. Yes to opportunity, yes to life. That is how Assets for Life was created.

And in just over two and-a-half years, we've been able to add £12.2 million worth of property to the portfolio, raise over £4 million in joint venture finance. Together in a partnership of equals with a broad skill base we've created an amazing business. We're a boutique property investment company but also we are in the education business too. Because we're a boutique, we are exclusive, which enables us to work with people on a very personal and deep level - why?

Because we want to share our knowledge with you, we want you to achieve amazing things both in life and in property.

So there it is, a potted history of me, of how I met Jay and how we set up Assets For Life. The point is, maybe you have lost a business or maybe you're not in the best financial position, it really doesn't matter. I'm here to tell you that wherever you're at, by making a decision to become a property investor, following the system in this book, you can achieve financial freedom, one property deal at a time.

So, what do you think? Am I a straight up guy? I've taken a few knocks; I've made some mistakes but look at me now! Back in the saddle and building my empire. And I did it by developing a system, which I call The No Money Down Blue Print. Now it's your turn. You are just six steps away from financial freedom. Here they are.

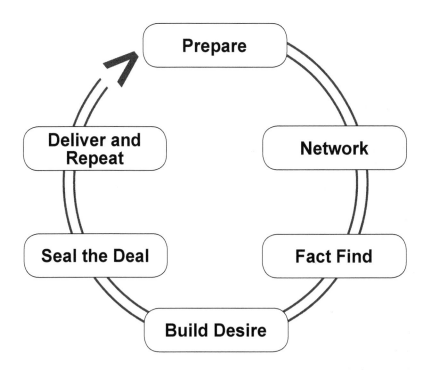

Going forward as you read the book I will take you through each of the steps in detail. As you will see, each step is multi-layered, with very simple actions that you will need to implement and follow. I want you to start preparing right now for your new future. I want you to get your first joint venture partner over the line relatively quickly, and to get your first or next property deal into the portfolio.

For that to happen, please understand that for the six steps to have any effect you must do this stuff.

This is where the work starts! So roll your sleeves up and let's get cracking. If you follow this system in the order that I'm going to explain it to you, by the time you've finished this book you are going to be in a position to start raising joint venture finance.

So, are you ready to take the first step?

Step One

Prepare

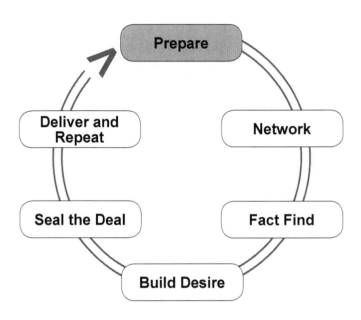

In this step you will learn all about:
Mindset
Building your brand
Your Values - Your Vision - Your Mission
Understanding The JV
Developing your investment products

Chapter 3

Mindset

Every action you take is based on a thought.

The way you think determines the way you act.

Now, before we get started, before we discuss anything else, the most important thing in business and in property is your mindset.

Have you ever thought about how you think?

In her book, Time To Think, Nancy Kline makes a stunning observation when she writes, 'The quality of any decision you take is based on the quality of thought preceding it'.

Most of us, me included, can spend our whole lives forgetting that we are in charge of the brain in our head and that while most of the time it does an awe-inspiring job occasionally we have to actively choose how to think and not just let the thinking happen.

Sometimes, to get the best out of ourselves and our business, we need to marshal our thoughts, challenge them and, indeed, change the way we think them.

Mindset is always something that tends to get missed when constructing a business strategy. But I promise you right now, when you are starting out in the property game you can read as many books as you like, you can listen to as many audio CD programs that you like, you can attend as many courses as you like, but if you haven't got the correct mindset, you're going to go round and round in circles and fall pray to your old ways of thinking. For example are you an optimist or a pessimist? Is the glass half full or half empty? Are you a positive thinker or do you suffer from an unstoppable stream of negative thoughts?

Spend a moment to look back on your life. Were there opportunities that you let pass you by because you 'thought' you weren't up to the challenge? What could have happened if your thinking had been different? What would have happened if you 'thought' you were up to the challenge?

Henry Ford the founder of Ford Motors one famously said, 'If you think you can or you think you can't, you're right'. The power of thought is immense so let's start to harness the power of your thoughts right now.

The mindset guru and keynote speaker Michael Hepple says, 'I'm not a big fan of positive thinking, I'm a big fan of positive doing'. So let's do something now to enhance you mindset for the challenges ahead.

I want to share with you an exercise that was given to me a few years ago, and it completely changed everything for me.

Back in the day when I was working all around the world I used to be a prolific networker and I spent a lot of time with a lot of people who had a lot of money. I'm talking millionaires and multimillionaires. Now, some high achievers are not interested in helping others, they want to keep success all to themselves but others, indeed most in my experience, want to share their knowledge to anyone who will listen so that they can succeed too.

One time I was invited to a yacht party being thrown by a hugely successful businessman that I had come to know. After about an hour or so we got chatting together and he kindly asked how things were going with my current enterprise. As I was describing all that was going on, what was going well what not going so well he stopped me. "Liam," he said, "I've got a surprise for you." And took me off into a room below deck away from all the hubbub of the party.

You can imagine what I was thinking, 'Blimey, this guy's about to give me a Rolex, maybe one or two gold rings. Better still, he's going to cut me in on one of his global business deals'!

We went into this little cabin. He sat me down, looked me square in the eye and said, 'Are you ready for your surprise?' By this point I was practically salivating with anticipation at the thought of what my surprise was going to be. I said, 'Go for it Richard'. And then he said this:

'You will never achieve the success you want. It will always be just out of reach and you are destined to spend the rest of your life never knowing why'. And do you know what I said? All I could come up with was, 'Oh. I thought you were going to give me a Rolex or something'. At which point he laughed like a drain and gave me a hearty slap on the back. "You can get your own Rolex." I said, 'Can I?' 'Yes,' he said, 'but you need to believe in yourself', I said 'do I?' he said, 'Yes, because you don't at the moment.' I said, 'Don't I?' He said, 'No. You think you do but you don't. Listening to you talking about your business just now, I can see you have huge potential but to achieve that potential you need to change your mindset.'

Mindset. That word again.

He went on, 'Look, you have a few mental blocks that are getting in your way. I can see they are affecting what decisions you take and I can also feel how they are having a negative impact on your self-esteem and overall energy levels. Are you up for a challenge?' I humbly said that I was. 'Good', he said and gave me another hearty slap on the back, which, incidentally, I was starting to wish he'd stop doing.

"'Liam, here's a pen, here's a piece of paper. Now I want you to sit here and make a list of the top 50 great things about you and your business." I was like 'wow 50 things! He said, "Take your time. Just start writing some stuff down and don't come back on deck until you've got those 50 things OK?'

It was amazing. I took up the pen and while the noise of the party was going above deck I got on with my task. I sat there for a full three hours. Suddenly I realised I couldn't hear the party anymore. Everyone had gone home. I folded up my list, put it in my jacket pocket and gingerly made my way upstairs. My host was sitting on his own looking out to the sunset. 'Liam! How did you get on? Did you get all 50?' 'Nearly', I said. He said, 'Great, how many did you get?' 'I said, 'Six'.

Once again he roared with laughter and once again he slapped me on the back. 'Don't worry. You'll get them. Carry that list around with you over the next few days and just be aware of everything that you do fantastically well, all the benefits you bring to your customers, all the things that make your business unique and special. As you think of them write them down'.

I soon made the list of 50 great things about me and my business. I think it took another day or so and when I looked at it and really thought about it I realized that what I held in my hand was worth more to me than ten Rolex watches. What I was holding had a value that money could not buy. I was holding the treasure that would go on to unlock my thinking and the mental blocks that previously stood in my way? They vanished into thin air. From that day I realized I've got something really valuable to give.

Don't listen to the monkey!

Have you got a monkey? I used to have a monkey and I carried it with me wherever I went. And what was amazing about this little monkey was that he could talk. In fact he never stopped talking and I used to listen to every word he ever said and I can remember what he said word for word.

'You're not good enough'

'No one in their right mind is going to give you money for JV'

'This is a waste of time'

'What's the point of doing this?'

'What's the point of doing that?'

'What's the point of doing anything?'

'No one's interested in you'

'No one believes in you'.

Those were the blocks that my back-slapping friend was on about. But once you have that list, the 50 great things about you, you can then put your best foot forward at any given time. It means that you can give yourself worth and value and carry yourself with dignity, pride and purpose. It's time for you to say goodbye to your monkey.

Think on Paper

So what I'd like you to do is get a pen and paper and I'd like you to write down 50 great things about you and your business and I want to then keep that on you at all times. Maybe use it as a screensaver on your computer, put it on your phone, put it next to your bed, read it every night, and by doing this very simple exercise, your confidence is going to increase and that is going to put you in a position where you can then go and raise a joint venture finance.

Old Thinking

Now you might be in position at the moment where you've got some old money beliefs. Maybe you were taught to work really hard for your GCSE grades, to work even harder for your A' levels and to put yourself in debt just to have the privilege of slaving over your studies to get a degree.

Then you get to put yourself in the highly competitive work market and get yourself a job for life. For the next 40 years you get a corporate job and work up the corporate ladder so that you can finally retire on a decent pension - well, we know how that goes. Sadly, for many, the foundations of that socio-economic structure have long since crumbled.

In my view, to start your working life with a debt of £50k hanging over you before you've even got going is scandalous. The whole notion of a job for life vanished in the mid 90s and most people's pensions aren't worth a thing.

So what is needed?

A new mindset!

Certainly in the last five years or so I believe there has been a massive shift in people's beliefs and thinking. People are slowly waking up to the fact that times are changing. That is why now there are more entrepreneurs of all demographic groups and backgrounds.

And from the point of view of you and your property portfolio the great news is there's more money then there has ever been. And, for reasons that I will explain later it is now easier to raise money than ever before and easier to gain massive returns than ever before.

In many ways you should consider yourself very fortunate indeed to have made the decision to create your own property portfolio at this time.

We are entering a time where people are desperately looking to invest their money to guarantee a half way decent pay back. People are becoming more daring, more creative and more ready to take their money out of the bank and put it to work for them. And you can help them do that. You can be the person to bring them in to something which is very special and extremely profitable for both you and your investor.

Believe me when I say this; in literally three years from now you can be in a position where you have built a multimillion pound business, but you have to have the mindset, you have to believe in yourself. Everything in property requires dedication, there is no get rich quick scheme here, but it is get rich slowly and as long as you follow the systems, you will achieve the goals that you want to achieve.

So if you are lacking some confidence at the moment, watch some motivational videos on YouTube, read or listen to some audio books. You could even check out my podcast, 'Liam Ryan, The Deal Maker'. You won't regret it, I promise. You'll be just one of literally tens of thousands of people globally to have heard it. In fact, on the day of its launch the podcast reached number six in the worldwide business podcasts - it even got higher than Tony Robbins! Another great way to get some positive energy is to go and start hanging out with people that are making money and doing what you want to do. Go and become inspired by your peers, by your mentors. This is something that I've been doing now for almost three years and it's completely changed everything for me.

Remember, what we think on the inside creates what we do on the outside. It's all in the mindset!

This Stuff Works – Dorian Payne on Mindset

Before I was mentored by Liam Ryan, I had a narrow mindset to raising money. I thought I had to do everything, work hard, save and recycle my own funds. After some intensive training and equipped with my new set of skills, I hit the ground working smart instead of hard. I had all of the required tools, assistance and support to raise money for my projects and allow investors to get a better return than they had previously received. To date I have raised just over £1,000,000 in finance for my projects and businesses. I have also benefited from a new business partner, after an introduction from Liam. Hopefully this book will be worth that for you. Best of luck and enjoy the journey.

Dorian Payne - Property Trader, Investor and Developer
Elidor Group, Taylor & Payne Group

Chapter 4

Building your brand

Treat this like a hobby and it will pay like a hobby.

Treat it like a business and it will pay like a business.

This is a business that you are building for the long term so you need to be properly prepared. Just like a house, your business needs to be built on firm foundations. There will be a few mistakes to learn from along the way, that's life, but we at Assets For Life have saved you from making a great deal of those mistakes because we made them first!

Jay and I are so passionate about what we do. We've worked extremely hard to get to where we are now. And we love sharing our knowledge and experience with you so you can go and do the same stuff – but hopefully without as many hiccups along the way.

As I'm sure you know, if you learn something from every mistake you make it turns from being a mistake into a valuable learning experience. Well Jay and I had a steep learning curve when we started out making mistake after mistake but we learnt from them so now, you can learn from us.

One of your key foundation stones will be education.

It is really important for you to get the right education in property. And the best place to go for this, in the first instance is online. I said earlier that I am the more public face of the company well, if you don't already know what I look like the good news is that you can hop onto our Assets For Life Facebook page, join the AFL property community Facebook group and check out just what a handsome fellow I am! We also have a hugely popular YouTube channel full of great info to give you a broad overview of life as a property magnate.

We also provide online webinars and online training sessions, all with a view to providing free content to you so you can enrich your understanding and educate yourself on all the different options and strategies that are available. We run world class property and business training events and have the AFL academy which is a year long mastermind/mentorship accountability programme.

For now, let's give you an idea of all the different product options there are for you. So you've got:

HMOs

House in multiple occupation also knows as a multi let is where a property is rented out by the room rather than to a single person/family. A HMO will increase cash flow and Return On Investment (ROI). A typical 5/6 bedroom HMO will generate £750 to £1,500 net profit per month . You can buy property to do this strategy or do it on a rent 2 rent basis.

Land development

A developer will buy a piece of land with or without planning and then build houses, flats or commercial units.

Commercial conversions

A developer will buy a commercial building such as an office and covert it into flats.

Lease options

This is where you can rent a property from a landlord and have an option at some point in the future to buy the property at an agreed price now. You have the option but not the obligation.

Service accommodations

Serviced accommodation is fully-furnished accommodation available for short term as well as long term stays. It provides hotel-like accommodation but with a home from home feel and is charged by the night.

Flips

A flip is where you will buy a house or a flat, carry out a refurb and sell it for a higher price than you paid it for. So you are trading property rather than holding property. This is good to build up a pot of cash.

Single lets
A single let is where you will rent out a flat or house to an individual, couple to family using a contact knows as ASTs, Assured Shorthold Tenancies.

If your head is spinning with all that just remember you don't have to do all of the above. What the list represents is choice. It gives you as the person building a portfolio a very important thing. It gives you options.

It's true that there are so many things to be thinking about and it's easy to start feeling a bit overwhelmed, but relax, you're in safe hands. One of the things that we offer at Assets for Life is our three day property millionaire's boot camps where we deep dive into every investment option I just talked about.

Right now though, as long as you are clear on one thing it will all fit into place and make perfect sense - your strategy. As long you're clear on what strategy (or strategies) you're going to be using you will move forward with a clear goal to aim for.

Two strategies for you to use
Now don't make the mistake that we made back in 2015. At the beginning of Assets For Life we decided we were going to do everything and I mean everything.

A favourite phrase of mine is 'Go big or go home' so we decided to go really big!

Yep, we were going to become nationwide deal packagers, we were going to go and do 40-50 unit conversations and at the same time we were going to go and raise £10 million in our first year. EASY!

Not!

It was great to have those aspirations and in truth we were making the rookie mistake of trying to run before we could walk. Yes, we wanted to take over the world but, as we found out, world domination takes time.

There was no doubt that we were committed but the lesson we learnt was that you simply can't do everything right at the start. Over time you're going to be building what is called 'multiple streams of property income', but I believe that for where you are right now you should focus on two strategies at the beginning:

Strategy 1

Is going to be a high cash-flowing strategy, so you can do the rent-to-rent model using service accommodation or multi-lets. For this you can raise joint venture finance and you can acquire the properties.

This strategy will quickly enable you to replace your income by generating passive income so, if you want to you can sack the boss or go part time. When you can get passive income through property your life will change very fast. What do I mean by passive income? Simply this; doing the work once and then investing very little or no time at all for the money to keep coming in!

Strategy 2

At the same time you can start thinking about doing your first big development. Maybe that's going to be a commercial conversion where you're going to take an office, maybe 4,000 square foot and convert that into six to eight apartments, maybe you're going to find a piece of land and you're going to build your first one or two houses, flats or bungalows.

The important thing is when working these two strategies is cash flow and then focusing on big lumps of cash.

It might be that while you are looking for change and new opportunities for growth, you actually love your job, earn good money and replacing income is not the most important motivator for you. That's fine, you could play the slightly longer game and start using JV finance for bigger deals.

Chapter 5

Your Values - Your Vision - Your Mission

So let's keep talking about foundations - business foundations.

Did you know that most new businesses fail within the first one to three years. A lot of business analysts are paid hundreds of thousands of pounds to figure out why this is the case. Well, here's what I think and you can have this for free. In my view, any business that fails in its infancy has suffered from a fatal lack of intellectual preparation. Which is a very wordy way of saying you have to get your head in the right place before you even start.

We have already discussed your WHY to get you going.

Now we need to talk about the development of something that will be crucial to keep you going. In the next few pages, together we are going to create one of these: your philosophical framework for success. I'm no mindreader but can I take a guess at what you're thinking right now?

You're thinking, 'Liam, why are we bothering with any of this? We just want to get on with it don't we? We want to start digging deep into how to create that million quid that you keep going on about don't we?' Was I close?

Well, I'm going to say something now that might surprise you.

It can't just be about the money.

The money will come but first you need to spend a little time thinking a few things first.

I'm about to ask some questions now that may not have occurred to you to ask of yourself. But the answers to these questions will put you leaps and bounds ahead of your competitors.

What are your values?

What do you stand for?

What do you stand against?

What is your vision?

Where are you now and where are you going?

So what is the vision for your business and ultimately what is your mission?

If this all feels a bit 'woo woo' I'm going to ask you one more question.

Have you heard of this lot?

Google

McDonald's

Microsoft

Apple

That's right, all the big blue-chip companies have spent a great deal of time making decisions about what their values are, they have a clear mission statement and a clear vision of what they want to achieve and it hasn't done them any harm has it?

Now you don't have to get it perfect at the beginning and your statement, your vision, mission and values may change over time, but it's really important to think about this and get something down on paper as a starting point.

So now I'm going to share with you the core values, vision and mission of Assets for Life to give you an idea of where we're at.

And when you have read through them, I'll ask you to create your own!

Our Values

We have six core values in our business and they are:

Quality

We strive for the very best quality in everything we do: the products we create, all our communications and publications. We will never compromise on this as we want our mentees, investors and eventual tenants to know that Assets For Life continually works at the very highest standard.

Trust

Trust is a vital commodity to us. If people trust our working practices they will trust us with their money. We aim to be scrupulously honest in all our communications with all the members of our team and anybody we come in contact with through our business. Our word is our bond.

Partnership
Anybody who comes on board with Assets For Life will come in with the understanding that we are a partnership of equals. Each person has a voice and a view that deserves to be heard and considered.

Respect
We will treat everyone with the utmost respect and dignity. Each person is on their journey, each person is doing their best at any given time and whether they decide to invest or come on board as mentees or choose not to they are people of equal value.

Dedication
We are 100% dedicated to the success of Assets For Life. We are 100% dedicated to the success of our mentees and investors – their success is our success.

Inspiration
Part of what we provide our mentees and investors is the inspiration to achieve incredible things. We want the people around us to have incredible ideas, develop the courage to stay up when the chips are down and ultimately inspire us to learn from their success be inspired by them.

So why are values so important?

When I was a young man I was making a few decisions that, to be honest, weren't that morally sound. They were good in the short term but I was putting myself and my business first above other things that were actually more important to me.

I'll never forget the day my Dad took me to one side, 'son, I need to talk to you about your moral compass'. I said, 'Why?' He looked at me with great compassion in his eyes as he said, 'because, at the moment, I can't help feeling it is pointing you in the wrong direction'.

It knocked the wind out of my sails to hear him say that. We talked for ages about the consequences our decisions have, not just on ourselves but those around us, those we love. From that day forward I made the decision to always do the right thing in my business and in my life.

I'm sad to say, my Dad is no longer with us but his legacy lives on in me every day in each decision I take.

Well, you are going to be faced with decisions that you are going to have to make in your business over the up and coming weeks, months and years. Sometimes those decisions are not always easy to make, sometimes you're going to be faced with working with some joint venture partners and you're not quite sure if its the right fit but you want their half a million quid!

Basically, whenever you have a difficult decision to make, and that may well happen on a daily basis, and you're not sure which way to go, refer back to your core values, they will help to guide you to a decision you will be both happy and comfortable with.

A good rule of thumb is, if it's in line with your core values then its probably a good decision to make.

Your core values provide you with a cross between a code of practice and a moral compass and over the days, weeks and years to come they will guide you away from the pitfalls and steer you to great success.

Our Vision

Financial freedom through property education and investment to live the life of your dreams.

We're all about living a life of abundance. We carry with us the awareness that we've only got one life and we have a responsibility to live it to the full. We will never know when our time is up so we are dedicated to achieving our dreams?

Are you living your life to the maximum? Are you enjoying yourself? Are you doing the things that you want to be doing? If you're not, take heart, you're just one decision away, one JV partner away, from something completely different. When you have completed your dream life I want you to read it back to yourself and understand one thing:

This is all possible. By using my system and raising JV finance your dream life can become a reality. Sometimes people fear success because they don't want to be judged. Well, people are going to judge you whatever you do or whatever you don't do so go for it! Turn your dream life into an amazing here and now. Enjoy success to the max but just promise me one thing –when you become a millionaire – don't become a dick! The world has enough of them already. Let your success help you to be more kind, more generous and more genuine. Inspiring stuff isn't it!

Think on paper
Here's a question for you: What is your dream life?

For me it's time being with my kids, taking them to school reading them a bedtime story, six holidays a year, fast cars, enjoying the benefits of owning luxury items, helping others, being successful and never having to worry about money.

I want you to take a few minutes to write down your dream life, don't hold back, and don't think small - think big.

Our Mission
Our mission statement is:

To share our knowledge and experience to help you prosper from the property market, to be the most effective, approachable property educational and investment company in the UK, and to create 10,000 millionaires.

That is the mission, and if we follow our mission it is going to get to our vision. Once we get to our vision, we're going to be able to leave a great legacy for our children and our children's children, and one day at a time were going to have a really positive impact on the world, to help people achieve financial freedom.

Our Legacy Statement
To be remembered for having a positive impact on the world and for Assets for life to carry down to our children and grandchildren.

Think on paper

I want you to put some time aside now for you to consider what are the three to seven core values of your business. So turn off your mobile phone, switch off your emails and do not allow yourself to be distracted. Do not rush this process. Let this thinking process take as long as it takes.

Write down the core values of your business and give a short description of why those values have meaning for you, just as we did on the pages above. Then I want you to spend time to consider your vision, your mission, YOUR OVERALL LEGACY. Write out a really punchy one liner for your vision and a more detailed description for your mission.

And when you have compiled all of those three things, write them up on a big piece of paper and put it on the wall of your office next to your list of ten things you want to achieve. This is a wonderful moment, as you will start to see the foundation stones of your business literally taking shape before your very eyes.

Other things that you're going to need to be thinking about:

What does your company do?

What strategy are you going to focus on?

One of the things we decided on right at the very beginning of Assets For Life was that we wanted to raise joint venture finance.

So we positioned ourselves as a boutique property investment company, we put together a very cheap but very effective four page website, because again that built our confidence and it made us look more credible.

We created our company Facebook page and then we went and got our business cards done; and we did all of this for less than £100. The beauty of what you are creating is that the initial start up costs are minimal.

By now you should have your values, vision mission and legacy laid out before you. You have now created your very own, bespoke philosophical framework for success. Well done. Feels good doesn't it? I cannot stress strongly enough the importance of laying these foundation stones to your business. Think about it. You are about to embark on an amazing journey where you're going to start meeting investors, raising capital and achieving all your dreams while helping others to achieve theirs.

It is an amazing thought isn't it? A fantastic new business enterprise with you at the helm reality but it is also quite a responsibility so...

Know who you are, know what you stand for and know what you want to achieve.

So now with your values, vision, mission and legacy in place you can get to work on your website, get to work on your Facebook page and get yourself a business card.

You're going to need all those things for what is coming up next.

Chapter 6

Why JV?

So, what is a joint venture?

Well the definition of a joint venture is 'a business arrangement in which two or more parties agree to pool their resources for the purpose of accomplishing a specific task'.

So, when we're talking about joint ventures with JV partners, they've got the money, all the money. Remember our business model is called the no money down blueprint. If our JV partners are pooling all the money, what recourses are we putting into the pot? Why don't they just get out there and build their own portfolio?

Because they don't have what you have - or will have very soon!

You've got the system

You've got the time

You've got the deal

You've got the passion

You've got the education

When the joint venture partner lends you money or invests money into a project that is their job more or less done. At this point however, your job has only just begun. You then you go and do all of the work to create a win-win situation for both parties.

They invest their money, you invest your time and expertise and you both come out the other side of the deal having made a lot of money. They're happy, you're happy. What you've got to remember is that a joint venture must be a win-win, it cannot be a win for them and a lose for you, or vice versa. Both parties must come out on top.

The ideal joint venture is where you arrange a meeting with someone who has a certain amount of cash and they agree to hand it over to you. Simple! No? Not simple? Well, maybe not simple but nowhere near as hard as you might think. It all depends who you want to listen to, me or your Monkey!

I bet that monkey on your shoulder has started piping up hasn't he? 'It'll never happen', 'This guy's a nut', 'Who's going to give you money?' 'And 'No one's got money that kind of money anyway'. Take it from me, your monkey is wrong, your monkey is mistaken, your monkey is a liar!

Don't get me wrong; I know where you're coming from. A few years ago when I started to think about the concept of joint ventures, I was listening to people in the property world talk about raising joint venture finance, and just like you, the first thing that I thought was 'that's a load of rubbish, no way can you do that. No one's going to give me any cash'. But look where I am today.

The point I'm trying to make is that you have a choice. You can go off and sit in a corner and listen to your monkey or you can listen to me.

Trust me when I tell you and there is just so much cash out there you wouldn't believe it. There is not shortage of cash. Getting cash is the least of your worries.

We're in a period, as well, of very low interest rates. Right now, as you are reading this, there are people are sitting on a lot of capital which is stuck in their bank and they are panicking because they're loosing money. Any money that is currently sitting in a bank account is a depreciating asset because of the rate of inflation. On top of that ISAs aren't performing as well as they should. Where else can people go to make their money work for them? Well, they could go to the stock market but a lot of people don't want to get involved because of the current global economic volatility.

You represent one of the best and ways of helping people to sort out this problem.

You!

You will be offering them an opportunity to JV where they can get a fixed rate return of 6, 8 or 10% a year! Compare that to any bank and what you are offering blows them out of the water. When they find out what you have to offer it will very quickly start to look like a no brainer.

What are your thoughts?

If you are still struggling to believe me you need to question your money mentality.

Don't have a scarcity mentality, have an abundant mentality because I'm telling you now there are millions of billions of pounds all over the place.

I'm not a religious man but I'm going to use a quote from the Bible:

'Seek and you shall find'

Can it really be that simple? If you look for a JV partner you'll find one?

Let's try a quick experiment. It's a memory test. Get a pen and paper and look round the room you're sitting in and I want to you take 30 seconds to try and remember everything brown in that room. Be strict, 30 seconds only and no cheating.

Once you've done it I want to you to go into another room as quickly as you can and write down as many of those brown items as you can remember.

Do that now!

If you have finished writing your brown things list, well done. I'm pretty sure you'll have quite a number of things on that list. Now, stay exactly where you are and write down a list of all the blue things in that room that you can remember.

Do that now!

Not such a long list is it? It might well be that you have nothing on that list at all, correct?

So what have we learnt here? It's simple. You will always find what you are actively looking for and will not see what you are not looking for even if it is sitting right under your nose. So decide to actively start looking for JV partners and you will start to find them. They are out there in huge numbers.

Not only are JVs plentiful in number but every one is every single joint venture is slightly different, unique in fact. This is because you are dealing with a different person each time and different people have different needs, different wants, different desires, and its for you and your investor to find out what works.

So the good news is a joint venture is like a blank piece of paper, and over a period of phone calls, emails, meetings, you and your investor will find a solution that is going to work for everyone.

So can I assume that you can see the brilliance of JVs as a business model, yes or no?

At this point in my seminars I ask that question and I see an ocean of hands go up because they have seen the light. There are, however, one or two lost souls who still haven't got my message. Sometimes I will get a lonely little voice pipe up saying, 'But how can I do this if I haven't got any money?' Let's deal with this question once and for all. If you've got no cash, I want to say one word to you right now.

Hallelujah!

Because do you know what? In my view it is actually sometimes easier for people with no cash to raise joint venture finance than it is with people that have got half a million pounds in the bank, because they're hungry, driven and focused on the challenge at hands. Let's face it, if you are sitting on half a million quid where's the need? Where's the desire? Where's the hunger?

I'm sincerely hoping that having no money, is going to be the catalyst, that deciding factor, that kick up the backside you need to go out and make a great success of raising joint venture finance. Remember to get something different, you have to do something different. And if you want change, you have to change.

So oddly, if you've got no cash, you're in a very, very good position. I might go as far as to say it's the best position to be in actually.

And if you're still not convinced about the power of the JV I want to leave you with this thought:

How does 50% of an asset sound, using none of your own money? I don't know about you but I'd much prefer 50% of something than 100% of nothing.

So, on that note, I'm going to take it as read that you are now on board and that you want to do joint ventures so you can start doing no money down deals.

Great decision.

One of the other great things about doing joint ventures is that you get to work together as a team with your investors. Property can be a lonely business if you're a one man or one-woman band, stuck in the office all day, looking at your spreadsheets all on your todd. Well at least if you've got one investor, it forces you to communicate with someone in the outside world, it forces you out of your comfort zone.

Of course, when you start doing joint ventures you're going to be able to scale a lot quicker than if you used your own cash, and it's all about getting that first or next joint venture partner over the line. And once you start you doing joint ventures there will be an endless supply of cash coming to you.

You might not quite think like that now, but believe you me, once I'm finished with you and once I've helped you go and get your first joint venture partner you will soon develop an abundant mentality that will continue to support rapid growth in both your portfolio and income.

But ultimately, what is really great about doing joint ventures is that not only does it benefit your life and your family but we get to help other people. We get to help our friends, family members, colleagues and business associates. We have the opportunity to help them get their money working for them so that they achieve their goals. One of the greatest pleasures I get through my work with Assets For Life is to see those around me prosper.

How to keep your investors on side
So some top tips that I want to share with you now:

Please make sure that every single month you are having an investor catch up - Skype, phone call, FaceTime.

Make sure that you're putting time in the diary to go and meet your investor and make it fun for yourself too. Go and eat at your favourite restaurant, play a round of golf or if you'd like a spa day, have a spa day! Go and treat yourself to a nice massage and facial and sit in the jacuzzi for an afternoon.

It's all part of the job!

Please build rapport with your new and existing investors, it's vital. Take time out to go and enjoy one another's company, not only will this deepen your relationship but it will encourage your investor to come back time and time again.

What does your JV investor want from you?

The one thing you have to project is confidence. If you have confidence in yourself your investor will have the confidence in you - they need to feel comfortable in making that all-important investment.

Just to remind you in the early days of Assets For Life, I'd just lost £392,000 in a renewable energy business, I'd been a part time, amateur investor in property but really I was a total novice. I was like you are now, about to try and get my fist JV investor. Do you think I felt confident? I'm going to surprise you now because yes I did! I felt supremely confident. Why?

Because I focused on my amazing list of the 50 great things about me that I had started to write on that boat all those years ago.

Go back to your list and read them out loud to yourself.

Do this now!

Isn't it a great feeling?

These are reason people are going to give you cash - because of everything that is brilliant about you. Sometimes it's easy to talk ourselves out of doing something because of what we feel we haven't got, because of things we don't have at our disposal. I need you to make the conscious effort to switch this around. You need to look at the assets you do have rather than the assets you don't have.

I'll ask the question again: What does your JV investor want from you?

An investor is looking for you to be credible

An investor is looking for you to be trustworthy

An investor is looking for you to be enthusiastic

An investor is looking for you to have the right education

An investor is looking for you to be part of a mentorship and mastermind programme

An investor is looking for you to have the right types of deals

And the good news is that and you have now started this process.

So I remember in the early days when I started to do this, I used to lean a lot on my mentors, I used to lean a lot on Jay and I leaned a lot on the fact that I had many, many years business experience.

Very rarely was I asked the question 'well how many properties do you have' or 'what have you done for other investors' because it's all done on trust, and that is why it's really important, like all things in property, to build that trust.

So why are people going to joint venture with you? There's many, many reasons, but let me just remind you of some of them:

By using the six-step system, you will be working from a place of experienced expertise.

You've got local knowledge, you're enthusiastic, and you've got passion.

You are going to have the winning deals.

You are going to do everything in your power to make sure that the money your investors give you, you are going to turn into a profit.

You are going to be providing an exceptional five star service.

You are currently in the process of gaining the education and know-how you need by reading this very book. But this book is just the beginning. It will stand you in great stead to get you going, no doubt about it but you might want to consider coming along to one of our hugely popular and highly impactful events.

We have a number of educational courses for you to choose from but I'd like to drawer your attention to just two right now. We hold a number of hugely dynamic events including The Property Investment Summit, which is a one day event. A two day course called The Property and Business Summit and The Property Millionaires Bootcamp which is our three day flagship event. Who knows, perhaps we will even mentor you one day and you will join the Assets for Life academy.

Of course no one is under any obligation to attend our events but I would say, even if you don't come a long to an Assets For Life event, seek out other opportunities. It's important to go and invest in your education, surround yourself with people raising money, be with people doing deals, have great mentors to guide you.

In this way you will be able to make an informed decision that this is what you want to do.

But the biggest reason as to why someone would joint venture with you is simply because you are you!

And you are highly investable. You are a great person, and you have a lot to bring to the table.

You've just got to go and believe in yourself. I guarantee 100% to show you how to get your first or next JV partner over the line.

Chapter 7

Developing your investment products

Now, we got our first ever joint venture partner over the line back in 2015. He was a guy called Dave. Dave lived in Basildon and we met him through a friend of a friend of a friend. I remember being introduced; I set up some meetings and had a couple of coffees.

Now, I've got a little confession to make. At that time I hadn't really prepared that much. I was just going out and meeting lots of people. I was full of adrenalin and positive mindset but at that time my education was lacking. However, what I did know was that the one way in which we could raise JV finance is though what's called a 'loan agreement'.

Another little confession? I have to admit that back then, every now and again I could still hear my flippin' monkey chattering in my ear. Every now and again there was this element of doubt that no one was going to give me cash to go and build a multimillion-pound property portfolio. Even as I turned up for my big meeting with Dave I kept thinking, 'can it really happen for me?' Well, I needn't have worried because it all worked out absolutely brilliantly.

I remember it like it was yesterday, after a series of meetings with Dave, he finally looked me in the eye, and he said "Liam, I love what you guys are doing at Assets for Life, we've met on a number of occasions, I am now ready to become one of your joint venture partners." The butterflies that I had in my belly, it was like it was Christmas day all over again. Then Dave said, "You know what I'm going to do, I'm going to invest £5,000 on a loan agreement." We shook hands and sealed the deal. Dave wanted a fixed rate return, so we'd agreed to pay a fixed 10% rate return. And boom! His money was now working for him and it was going to be working for us too. Win –win!

I have to say in all honesty, my heart sank a little when I heard the figure was willing to invest. I knew at this stage that he had a lot more money than £5,000, but the point is, it was a start. Whilst it wasn't the fortune I had been hoping for, it was enough to get Assets For Life up and running (we actually used that £5,000 to go towards a refurb of one of our multi-let refurb properties).

The truth is, the amount of money really didn't matter; we were on our way. I'd got my first ever JV partner! I remember feeling so excited. I jumped in my car and I raced home.

I arrived at the house and literally couldn't get out the car quick enough, I opened the front door and shouted out to my wonderful partner, "Holly, Holly, we've got our first joint venture partner. This really does work."

Holly rushed down the stairs and gave me a huge hug. In that moment I just felt so proud of myself. We immediately cracked open a bottle of bubbly and Red Bull for me. Holly prepared an amazing meal for us and I started to speak about our future full of optimism and an overwhelming sense of confidence that everything was going to be brilliant from here on in.

I called Jay. I said, "Jay we've done it, we've got our first investor over the line," he said, "brilliant," I said, "it's Dave from Basildon, I've been talking to you about him, he's going to loan us £5,000 on a fixed rate return". And Jay said, "that's great Liam, but £5,000 isn't exactly a fortune is it?" And I said, "no but I've got the solution," he said, "Go on then," I said, "we just need to go and find 100 Daves."

That moment when Dave committed to becoming an investor changed everything for me and Assets for Life and when you get your first or next JV partner over the line, you will know exactly what I am talking about.

The reality is you don't need 100 Daves. As I'm sure you know, it is better to have quality rather than quantity. Obviously Dave was a great investor but I remember thinking after that initial agreement with him that we had to put together a range of investment products that we can present our to our potential joint venture partners so that we weren't limited to just one offer when talking to would be investors.

When I put my mind to it two questions popped into my head. What type of joint venture partners do we want? And how can we capture as much as the market as possible?

So having Dave as our first investor was all that I needed in order to finally change my mindset. That first little deal gave me the confidence and the belief that I could now scale this part of the business. So with this in mind Jay and I sat down and had a brainstorming session and we created our Assets for Life products for our investors.

They have proven to be a hugely successful range of options for our investors and now I'm now going to share them with you. Yes, that's right, you can have this amazing intellectual property for the price of this book!

We want to save you the time and effort it takes to create your own products so just copy what we have done. We're not trying to reinvent the wheel, just follow the steps that I'm asking you to go and do and use these terrific investment products to kick off your property portfolio. I promise you will be amazed by the results.

Product Number 1 - The Assets for Life savings accelerator

This really is a loan agreement, and this is aimed at friends, family members, people you meet down the pub. This is perfect for people that are looking for a fixed rate return.

It might be that they've got some money in ISAs that are not performing or they've just pulled some money out of the stock market and they want a fixed rate return just like Dave from Basildon. They're not necessarily looking to become an equity partner in the deal, but they've got a bit of cash sitting in a bank somewhere and they don't know how to make it work for them.

Not a lot of people know that the any money in a bank is a depreciating asset, so once you point out to them they will be keen, indeed desperate to invest with you.

With the savings accelerator product an investor will loan you money, let's say £10,000. You will give them a fixed rate return on their capital invested. Again, let's say it's 10% because that's typically what we offer out to our investors, That might be for one year, and at the end of the year you then need to pay back the £10,000 plus the £1,000 interest - £11,000 in total.

At that point the investor has a few options. They can take back all the £11,000 and leave it at that, happy to have a made a quick grand or they might choose to pull out their profit and leave you with the original investment for another year or they might just invest the £11,000 and move into the second year.

The Assets for Life savings accelerator is a great product to build up some trust with your investor. It also helps you to build credibility and it's a great way for investors to dip their toe in the water without having to take any risks.

From your point of view there are many great benefits about the savings accelerator as an investment product:

It's easy

You can offer this out to any type of investor

You can get a loan agreement drawn up from your solicitor

NB: Everything is done through solicitors, all the KYC checks, anti-money laundering documents, so everything is there and everyone is protected.

When you're doing the Assets for Life savings accelerator product or your own version of that, some investors may require security. Depending on how much they're investing and what project you're going to use that money for, you have a couple of options.

You could give them second charge or first charge or you could get an RX1 which is a restriction on one of your assets which means you can't sell that asset unless that restriction has been taken off.

There's many ways in which you can offer security – however, my personal experience is that none of the investors we've got on the Assets for Life savings accelerator, have requested security. Why? Because the deals were based on trust and rapport building.

I once had to do a personal guarantee to a woman who loaned us £100,000 from a Small Self Administered Scheme (SSAS) but I was fine with that because I have total confidence in what we do.

Product number 2 - The Assets for Life Portfolio Builder

Now this is a much longer-term product for your investors to put their capital. This product is all about acquiring assets and holding those assets long term for the purpose of wealth creation.

Typically, we only offer this product out to high net worth and sophisticated investors. The reason for this is because the FCA (the Financial Conduct Authority) has a regulation known as 13/3, which basically says that if you are going to go into the property business with this type of product you need to set up a limited company. This is what we call a SPV - special purpose vehicle. This is where the investor will place all their funds. As you can see this is more of a complex structure for investment so it is really important that your would-be JV partner is high net worth or sophisticated.

I think that is the first time we have touched on the legalities and more on that later. But in the meantime check out this website which will basically tell you all you need to know: www.fca.org.uk/publication/policy/ps13-03.pdf

I know there are a few terms in there that might need a bit of explaining. After all it's good to have things clear right at the start. As explained by the FCA a sophisticated investor is a retail client with extensive investment experience and knowledge of complex instruments, who is better able to understand and evaluate the risks and potential rewards of liquid investments.

A high net worth client, on the other hand, has a number of criteria that will qualify them as such. For example, they must have an annual income of more than £100,000 or they must have a investable net asset of more than £250,000. These criteria are subject to review and can be updated in the future.

Back to the product:
So typically, the Assets for Life portfolio builder is where we will raise money with an investor, they will put in all of the money, we will go and do all of the work, we will hold the asset in a special purpose vehicle with the investor, and we will then recycle, refinance and look to recycle as much of the initial investment as possible, pay the investor back their initial investment and then split the profit 50/50 or the rental income 50/50, and then we own half of the asset with the investor.

So how does that sound to you? Take a moment to really think about the product I have just described.

With the Assets for Life Portfolio Builder you are enabled to build a property empire where you are owning 50% of assets yet you have not put a single penny in yourself! This is the Assets For Life magic at work. It sounds impossible but believe me it is more than possible if you use our process.

The Beauty of the Asserts For Life Portfolio Builder is that we do all the hard work while the investor can sit back and watch their money grow.

Depending on how much your client wants to invest, you can offer between 6% and 12% fixed rate returns per year- compare that to just 1% from the average ISA and 0.5% when people leave their money in the bank, it's easy to see why so many ambitious investors are choosing this fast track option.

Product number 3 - The Assets For Life Buy To Sell
This product is aimed at investors that want to invest into property deals but they don't want to hold the asset for say rental income. They want to do a development or a refurb, with a view to selling the assets and splitting the profit 50/50.

So, for example, you might go and find a property for £100,000. The property might need a full refurbishment, which costs £50,000, so the total invested by the JV partner is £150,000 including stamp duty and legal fees and all that type of stuff. So how do you make money on this?

When all the work is done and the refurb is completed you sell the property at its new market valuation, for the sake of argument say £250,000. When you sell this asset, the original £150,000 will go back to the investor and then you will split the £100,000 50/50 between you. Just to be crystal clear, that's £50,000 each!

Again, this is a great product where you can start to make big lumps of cash without using any of your own money.

This strategy is particularly popular with high net worth individuals, business angels and company directors who understand business and are attracted to large, exciting new projects.

Product Number 4 - The Assets for Life Complete Sourcing Solution

This is aimed at investors that don't want to split profits, give any equity or a share of the asset. How do you make money in this scenario? Simple, we charge a fee to the investor for sourcing the property, for doing the project management work.

If they are keeping the asset we will charge a further fee for managing the tenants.

So that's a great strategy where you can get in some cash flow in the first year or so. It is a great product for you to use as your start up. The likelihood is that you will quickly evolve away from this product.

We don't really do that anymore at Assets for Life. We did it in the beginning just as you will, but we've gone onto another level now and if we're going to work with joint venture partners, we're going to want 50% of the profit or we're going to want to own 50% of the asset once we have refinanced. Having said that The Assets for Life Complete Sourcing Solution was a vital part of our evolution.

Cash flow right from the start

Now, how can you get cash flow when you work with your investors? This is a question I get asked a lot and a question Jay and I asked each other right back at the start of Assets For Life.

I only wish we knew then what we know now. At the very start of Assets For Life it felt like we were doing all the work for free. Very soon, we were exhausted, frustrated and nearly skint! Confused and a little downhearted, we sought advice from one of our mentors and our mentor said, "you've missed a trick there, this is what you need to do."

The first thing you need to do is put a value on everything that you are bringing to the table. Namely:

Your time
Your services
Your knowledge
Your experience

And last but by no means least,

Your expertise

Make no mistake; you are bringing a great deal of value to the party so how do we price that? Well, this is what we do now and it is a highly effective way of getting cash flow at the beginning of each relevant project.

With all of our joint venture partners we will apply a sourcing fee to go and source a property, that's typically £5,000 for a multi-let or 1-3% of the purchase price of say a development.

Then, because we are going to become project directors during there build conversion phase, we will also apply a project management fee which could be anywhere from 2% to 15% of the build cost depending on the type of project.

So, not only are you making 50% of the profit at the end, not only are you owning 50% of the asset, but you can also get cash flow right from the beginning.

And that is the important thing about having a mentor. Their advice and guidance will save you money and make you money. In business and in property it is vital that you have someone who you can turn to and get all of the relevant help, support and guidance throughout your journey.

We want you to succeed in this journey. This is why we run the Assets for Life academy - it's a very high level 12 month mentorship mastermind programme where we will literally hold your hand day by day, step by step to ensure that you achieve great results.

So, remember having an investment product will benefit you both in the short term and the long term. And by creating a range of products you can offer your investor choice, if they don't like one option you can show them another and another. The more products you have the more likely you are to bring someone across the line.

That said, it is really important to understand how each of those products work, and that you have an individual 3 -4 page brochure on each of the products that you develop.

Since we created our product brochures, we have gone on to raise millions in joint venture finance and you can do this also. By having a well-produced piece of literature you raise the status of both yourself and your product. You can then show it to investors when you meet them at networking events or when you go and have coffees giving your more credibility and helping your to appear professional and businesslike.

And that is step one completed!

So just to summarise we've spoken about mindset, developing your products, vision, values, mission. We talked briefly about setting up a small website and getting your business cards sorted and we've spoken about the different types of products, services that you can offer out to your joint venture partners.

Step Two

Network

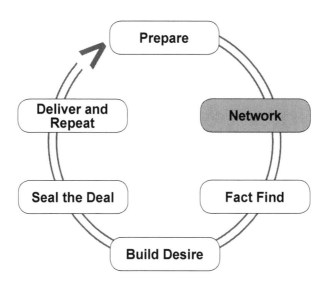

In this step you will learn:

What networking actually is!

How to prepare a killer 60 second pitch

Where to network

How to network

Case study from Chris Hopkins, one of our Asset For Life mentees

Social media

Chapter 8

What is networking?

So we've been talking about preparing your vision, your values, your mission, laying the correct business foundations, working on your business card, generating a small website and creating your product brochures. Now you need to know who to talk to about the incredible opportunities you can provide.

Firstly, you need to get to know your local area really well, go and build relationships with estate agents and go to a lot of property viewings. Go and speak to other investors in your area. That is going to give you confidence because you need to now KNOW what you're talking about when you go and meet investors of your own. Having local knowledge and good working relationships is going to show credibility and provide great social proof that you know the area in which you are asking them to invest into.

This is more of the groundwork I've been speaking about so much. And it is advice that you are getting for free that I paid a huge amount for. When I first got into property as a full time professional, I invested tens of thousands of pounds in education, mastermind programs and high-level mentorship.

One of the first things my mentor said to me was, "Liam, you've got to go networking." Up until that point, I had no concept of what networking was, how to do it or indeed where to do it. So just in case you are now like I was then, let me enlighten you.

The definition of networking is as follows:

'Networking is a supportive system of sharing information and services among individuals and groups having a common interest.'

In practical, real-world terms, it means going into a room full of strangers, speaking passionately about your business to all the people you meet. On top of that it will, most likely, involve giving a 60 second speech to everybody in the room where you speak uninterrupted about all your products and services.

...And if you are really serious about getting to know your local area you absolutely must go networking.

Yes, networking!

Are you starting to feel a bit queasy at the thought of all that?

Don't worry, that is a perfectly natural reaction. Once my mentor had explained all that networking entailed I initially just thought, 'There's no way I'm doing that! What are people going to think of me? I never speak to large groups all at once.' If those are the type of thoughts cropping up in your mind right now let me just say one thing:

Get out of your own way and make room for success.

Yes, networking can be a little nerve-shredding when you first start, but remember, life begins where your comfort zone ends. The first networking event I ever went to was in 2015 at the Chelmsford property-networking event and I certainly felt like a fish out of water. I had, however, made the decision to go and committed to attend no matter how nervous I was feeling.

I remember driving up to the Pontlands Park Hotel, it was about 6pm and, not to put too finer a point on it, I was absolutely crapping my pants. I had even developed a nervous twitch! I wasn't feeling too good at all. My palms were sweaty and I was feel very nauseous but, hey, but you've got to do what you've got to do, and to get something different, you've got to do something different.

I was definitely taking myself out of my comfort zone, which was where I knew I needed to be so; I took a deep breath and made my entrance.

I quickly got myself a coffee, and stood by a plate of biscuits comfort eating like there was no tomorrow. I was certainly that person in the corner of the room feeling quite nervous and quite scared and, after 20 minutes or so, quite full!

One of the great things about the people you meet on the networking circuit is how helpful and open they are. It wasn't long before I was being invited to engage in gentle social chitchat, which soon led the way for me to talk about Assets For Life.

Ultimately, the event went extremely well. I made some great contacts, and my confidence grew massively as the evening went on. Afterwards, I was like 'Wow, this is amazing. I'm in a room full of people I've never met before, all of whom want to listen to me speaking about my passion for portfolios.'

I suddenly had a blinding realisation.

To create business I have to put myself out there.

That's something that you need to remember. You've made the decision to go and raise joint venture finance, and that's great but I'm here to tell you that you're not going to wake up in the morning and have money just fall through your letterbox. There is money out there alright and it will come to you but you are going to graft for it. And a major part of that will be you going out and networking.

You're going to have to be seen and you're going to have to be heard. Yes, you'll be going a mile outside your comfort zone, but take heart, once you've done it once or twice you will grow to love it. Believe me, you'll soon come to enjoy the whole experience. This is a great way to build relationships and a fantastic way to make contacts that may well convert to becoming a business partner or your fist JV partner. Once these relationships start being created things will change for you very, very quickly.

So in this next section session we're going to be talking about a key ingredient to networking success and I'm going to give you some great actions to take forward that you can start implementing today to get you that step closer to achieving your financial dreams.

Chapter 9

The 60 second elevator pitch

I'm going to ask you a question now: do you have a 60 second elevator pitch nailed down?

I'm guessing maybe not, and if you don't, I must tell you, you're missing out on a trick. In fact, I'll go further than that, if you are going networking without a polished 60 second pitch, you may as well just stay at home, it really is that important.

So what is a 60 second elevator pitch?

Well, an elevator pitch is a short summary of who you are, what you do and how you can help someone, and typically it lasts from 40 seconds anywhere up to 60 seconds.

Why is it important in building your property portfolio?

Because you just don't know who you're going to meet that may have an interest in coming on board with you. Not only that, you don't know when you're going to that special person that want to know all about the investment possibilities of a JV. And if you do suddenly happen upon someone who want to know more, you don't want to become all tongue-tied when the moment comes for you to speak. You need to arm yourself with what is, in essence, a script so that you can come across as fluent, expert and passionate.

Here's a lovely little story. You know I said just you never know where or when you are going to meet an interested party? Well, as part of my drive for education around building my business I attended a presentation skills workshop at the end of 2015 that was specifically designed around creating your 60 seconds pitch. Well one by one we all had to get up and do our pitch. When it came to my turn, I've got to be honest with you, I was obviously feeling a bit nervous but I got up and did the best that I could.

Well, I must have got something right because in the tea break a wonderful woman called Pollyanna, came over to me and said, "Wow, I want some of that, I've been looking for someone like you for a long time." Result!

We booked in a coffee, spent some time together and Pollyanna became a joint venture partner where we purchased a property in Colchester that we converted into a six bedroom multi-let, a HMO for professionals. It just goes to prove my point that being in the right place at the right time is one thing knowing to say the right thing is key.

So, I'm now going to share with you exactly how to create your perfect 60 second elevator pitch.

Your elevator pitch, is broken down into four sections:

Section 1
Who you are

Section 2
What do you do

Section 3
How you can help

Section 4
A call to action

As a brief example of putting this list into a comprehensive speech I'm going to share my 60 second elevator pitch with you and the above list will start to make sense.

So, here goes ladies and gentlemen, this is my 60 second elevator pitch, and it goes something like this:

"Good evening everyone, my name is Liam Ryan and I am one of the co-founders of Assets for Life. Assets for Life is a boutique property investment company, we're based in the south east of the UK and we specialise in multi-lets, land development and commercial conversions.

"But what we really love to do is work with people like you to help you achieve freedom, to help you build a multimillion pound property portfolio, where you can start to live the life of your dreams that you deserve and desire. I love property, I love working with people like you.

So if you'd like to know more about Assets for Life and how we can help you achieve financial freedom, I'm going to be standing over by the teas and coffees in the break, come and say hi, lets connect and see what we can do, thanks very much."

This is something that I've been using now for three years and it has 100% set me apart from many other people on the networking circuit and it has certainly helped us raise over £4m in joint venture finance, which you are going to do as well.

Let's go through that speech again and I will point out the four component parts from the list.

Section 1
Who you are:

"Good evening everyone, my name is Liam Ryan and I am one of the co-founders of Assets for Life."

Section 2
What do you do:

"Assets for Life is a boutique property investment company, we're based in the south east of the UK and we specialise in multi-lets, land development and commercial conversions."

Section 3
How you can help:

"But what we really love to do is work with people like you to help you achieve freedom, to help you build a multimillion-pound property portfolio, where you can start to live the life of your dreams that you deserve and desire. I love property, I love working with people like you."

Section 4
A call to action:

"So if you'd like to know more about Assets for Life and how we can help you achieve financial freedom, I'm going to be standing over by the teas and coffees in the networking break, come and say hi, lets connect and see what we can do, thanks very much."

Now it's your turn.

Think On Paper

Put pen to paper and I'd like you to write down who you are, what you do, how you can help people, and a call to action. Now if you've not quite got your property business together yet practice on your current position in your work place or your current business. Again, it doesn't have to be right straight away. Practice makes perfect, write out the bullet points, then I want you to stand in front of the mirror and piece it together. Do This Now!

I want you to practice this five times a day for just 21 days. What a great thought that in just 21 days from today, you will have an elevator pitch nailed down which you can repeat time and time again. You will always be able to speak with confidence and fluency whenever people ask you what you do.

It is a fascinating thought that 90% of those who attend networking meetings admit to feeling uncomfortable when talking about their own business. 90%!

Be a part of the 10% of people speak with confidence and passion about what they do because they're the ones becoming the thought leaders and the go-to people at that networking event. They are the people going out there raising the money and they are the ones getting the deals.

Please understand, networking is a vital fundamental component of you becoming successful and living the life of your dreams that you deserve and you desire.

Not only that, and you might find this hard to believe right now but networking is going to become major part of your social life. It won't be long before you realise that the people you are meeting in the networking environment are going to become your friends as well as great business contacts.

So make a choice.

Rather than watching EastEnders on a Tuesday night, rather

than meeting your mates down the pub for a bag of crisps and a couple of pints, start going out to networking events and start hanging around where the money is.

If you put yourself in the company of people with money, once they know you, like you and trust you, they will give you capital to invest in your portfolio. So choose to put yourself in the right place at the right time saying the right thing to the right people!

Chapter 10

How to network

Now, there's one thing knowing that you need to network, but it's a completely story knowing how to network. Over the last few years I've been to hundreds of networking events and I see people doing it wrong all the time. I don't want you to follow the masses and do what most people do. It's easy to follow the heard but I want you to stand out for the exciting and energized individual that you are. Your uniqueness is what is going to make you stand out from the crowd.

Now what most people do is go to one networking event once a month in their local area. Wrong! That's certainly not enough in order to make any impact whatsoever. You simply won't be putting yourself in front of enough bodies to make the sufficient connections you need to raise the joint venture finance you will need to move forward in any meaningful way.

Another mistake they make is that they always go and speak to the same person that they spoke to the month before and the month before that. Why? - because it's the easy option.

Yes, it may be a pleasant opportunity for an informal catch up but it's not networking. Nothing will come of this sort of laid-back interaction. And while they are having their fill of all the coffee and pastries, they are not developing any new relationships; they are not reaching out to other people in the room.

It is exactly this sort of person who never stands up to do give a 60 second elevator pitch. They stay firmly in their seat, determined to take no risks and do nothing that is going to make them feel uncomfortable. But as Shakespeare so rightly said, 'Nothing will come of nothing'.

If you are going to go networking do it right, get out there and get involved.

I want you to network the right way, I want you to become a

leader, I want you leading from the front, I want you to inspire and motivate people to act, to invest, to get you on your way to financial freedom.

Remember business is all about putting your best foot forward, looking at the assets you do have rather than what you don't have.

If you still have the collywobbles about going to your first networking meeting go to your list of 50 great things about you and your business, it will inspire you.

So what I'm going to share with you now is going to be instrumental to the success of your property business.

This is a must do. Do this and you will get the very best out of your networking activities.

Here are some Key Performance Indicators (KPIs) to follow:

Attending at least one networking event per week. This is a minimum requirement, do more once you get used to it but at least one a week as a start up.

When you are at the networking event, introduce yourself to people! It's all too easy to be a networking wall flower. Avoid this like the plague.

I'm going to set you the challenge of introducing yourself to at least five people per session.

Now, you might not do this on the first one or two that you go to I understand that, but eventually you should build yourself up to the magic five handshakes. And with each of those people you want to spend in the region of five to ten minutes getting to know them.

When you're having your interaction take the opportunity to ask them such questions as "where are you in your property journey? What are you focusing on? What are you looking to achieve from your property journey?" While you're farming information and data from your new networking connection keep a few things in the back of your mind.

Is there some synergy here?

Do I feel I can help this person?

Is this person a potential JV opportunity?

Alternatively, is this the person that might be able to introduce me to an investor?

A big question to ask yourself is, 'Do I feel we can both benefit from building a relationship'. If the answer to that question is yes, then what I would like you to do is book in a coffee with that person there and then. Yes, right there and then, get our your phones and book in a coffee.

You might be thinking 'isn't that a bit pushy?'

It doesn't have to be.

You might say something along the lines of, "John, this has been an amazing conversation, it's really great to connect with you. I definitely feel there is some synergy between us, what does your diary look like for the next week or two as I would love to have a coffee, would that be ok with you?"

If you have picked someone with whom you have struck a genuine rapport they will most likely reply with, "Yeah no worries Liam, sure, let me get my diary out" - all good so far.

Then go on to book the coffee for the earliest possible opportunity where you are both available. I normally say one or to weeks.

You must never come across as pushy; people will feel that straight away and close up in an instant. So avoid saying "look let's meet tomorrow," but I'll bring my phone out and I'll try and get that coffee booked in for as quick as I can.

I might say something like, "what do you prefer John, Starbucks or Costa coffee? What does your diary look like for the next couple of days? When is the best time for you to be available?" and then book in the coffee.

Now, when you follow this system, and you go to one networking event per week, after just two months that's eight networking events you will have attended.

At each networking event you would have made contact with a minimum of five people, so that's 40 people now added to your database of other investors and like-minded individuals, and from those people you would have booked in at least 16 coffees.

Now, think about this for a few seconds, you go and have 16 coffees with like minded people, investors, entrepreneurs, do you think that you're going to raise investment? 100%!

So where do people go wrong?

They don't book in the coffees!

They might go from networking event to networking event with the best of intentions, they go and collect loads of business cards which go in the top draw the minute they get home. All of a sudden, a few months down the line they've got 100 dust covered business cards they were given by 100 people they can't even remember! Don't let this happen to you.

This is one of the best bits of networking advice I can give you. Ready?

Follow up! And by that I mean book in the coffees!

Doing this simple thing will reap huge rewards for you and justify all the time you have invested in networking. And If you follow the system I have just described I can guarantee it works.

Having said that, I recently had one of our graduates from the Assets for Life academy make a complaint!

He was one of our superstar attendees, committed, enthusiastic and willing to go the extra mile to achieve his dreams. He was doing a terrific job of going out networking so I was confident that it would only be a short matter of time before he started to clock a few JVs.

But one day he came up to looking really furious. "Liam", he said, "this whole networking thing is a total waste of time. I've been doing maybe three a week. I've spent quite a bit of money and a heck of a lot of time going round introducing myself to five people at each meeting and nothing is happening. It just doesn't work!"

For a moment I was stunned. I just didn't know what to say and then it occurred to me, "Are you doing the coffees?"

"No."

"Why not?"

"I forgot all about them! Oh, I'm a bit of a pratt aren't I?"

"Yes, mate you are!"

I said, "Look, here's what I want you to do. Stop networking for a while. I want you to get all the business cards you collected from people and, for the next few weeks, I want you to pick up the phone and call everyone you met and then do you know what I want you to do?"

"No," he said.

"BOOK THE COFFEES MATE!"

Well our star pupil followed this very simple process to the letter and guess what - he started to raise joint venture finance just as I said he would.

So there are some very important but simple key performance indicators to follow:

Start telling people everywhere you go about what you do and how you can help them. When you're on the train, when you're in the supermarket, when you're at your son's rugby match, anywhere and everywhere you go! Just start telling people what it is you do.

Soon you will start to position yourself as the expert. It might sound a bit fantastical now but this will happen. Why? Because you're going to have a vision, your values, and your mission.

You're going to have your products, you're going to get the education, your confidence is going to be growing, you will be attending lots of networking events, continually refining your 60 second elevator pitch, and you are booking the all important coffees.

I can not stress this enough, its the coffee where the magic happens.

One last valuable tip about how to network successfully- don't go with any real expectation, just go to serve and solve.

S + S = S that is serve plus solve equals success!

Just go with an open heart, and open mind and always be thinking 'How can I help this person,' because it's not about you, it's about them and knowing exactly what they want will then help you determine what you can do to help them to create a win-win and form a joint venture partnership.

This stuff works - Kate Sparsi on using KPIs

Since working with Liam my KPIs (key performance indicators) were to attend one networking event a week, to present a 60 second pitch about what I'm doing, pick up business cards and then convert those business cards into follow-up coffee meetings.

I have stuck to that formula religiously and it has worked fantastically for me. My business partner Marty involves himself in all the behind-the-scenes stuff while I'm the face of the business. I get out there and speak to people, build up relationships, find out what people want to see if we can help them.

The KPIs have helped remain firmly goal oriented and the results have been fantastic.

Kate Sparsi, co founder Assets 360

Chapter 11

Where to network

So where can you go and network? There are so many places where you can go and network, there really is no excuse not to.

Well here are some of the top places where you are going to go and find joint venture finance.

Do this now!

Type 4N Networking into Google. I guarantee you'll have a 4N Networking meeting within a ten-mile radius of you. It is an organisation where local small to medium sized business owners come together to create contacts and do business. They normally run them in the morning, occasionally in the afternoon and sometimes in the evening. Similarly type in BNI. This is a slightly stricter networking outfit but their members claim that the referrals-based group yields serious turnover.

You can also get yourself to property networking events and there's many hundreds of property networking events all over the UK on a week-to-week basis, so how are you going to find those? Well again, you can find most things on Google.

Type into Google 'property networking events in my local area' and you will get things like progressing property networking events, Pin networking events, independent networking events, and you can typically register your ticket and you can get involved for maybe £5, £10 or £20 which really is not a great deal of money at all.

Passive networking

Then there is what is known as 'passive networking'. What that basically means is doing the sort of things you like to do but talk about your business when the moment feels right. Think about local social clubs, book clubs or even the quiz night down your local. These are great places to bring up the JV model whenever the question 'so, what is it you do?' comes up.

Here's a good one, go and join your local social club. Think about it, Flying people that fly their own plane they tend to have quite a bit of money. Put yourself around those people who you think will have money and you will soon find an opening in the conversation where they are moaning about the current interest rate and boom, you're in!

You can go to business angel events, you can get down your local sports clubs, rugby clubs, football clubs, you can go to your local charity events, speak to your solicitor and see what charity events they are holding.

It's worth remembering of course your current friends and family members. I guarantee that someone in your personal network will have capital sitting in a bank, which is a depreciating value, and those people will be looking for somewhere else to place there hard earned cash.

Start reaching out to people.

Soon you will be talking them through what you do as a property investor developer. Once they hear your message you will start building confidence and building desire. And soon you will be building your client list.

Raising money in my opinion is not the difficult part around property, what we find more of a challenge is actually finding deals that stack up, and that's why its important to have a deal flow and also a investor flow because you don't really want to be in a position where you've got more deals than money and more money than deals, and what you want to try and do is balance the two up the best as you possibly can.

Don't hold back.

Ideally, you want to be going to at least one networking event on a week-to-week basis, make it a bit of a social. Go regularly and go often.

After going to my first property-networking event, I started to go to many networking events of all descriptions. It amazes me now when I think that I used to go to three or four events every single week.

I would always get to the networking event first and I would always look to leave last, because if you're investing your time for an evening or a morning, you want to make sure you make it as productive as you can to get the best possible result.

I just got out there, and I started to meet like-minded people, people that were looking to get a better return on their money. I was meeting professional investors within the property world, I was having lots of coffees, I was building rapport and I was building relationships where we could create a win-win situation.

And remember, I didn't go networking for the fun of it, I had a strategy and it paid off.

Chapter 12

Social Media

Now, another way in which you can get your message out there to the masses is through social media networks.

Many of the social media platforms, if used correctly, can be your biggest and cheapest marketing tool. The way we advertise today is very, very different to the way things were done five or ten years ago and the number of people now using Facebook, YouTube, Twitter etc. literally goes into the millions and the billions.

As of December 2017, Facebook has over 2bn users, an increase of 16% on the previous year. And if you think that's impressive, listen to this; YouTube has 30m users per day and 330m people visit Twitter every single month! These statistics are amazing and they represent and incredible opportunity for letting people know who you are and how you can help them.

Now the reality is if you are not active on social media you are going to be left behind over the up and coming weeks, months and years. Take me as an example; not so long ago I didn't even have a Facebook account! I hated social media, I hated Facebook, I didn't understand it, if the truth be known I was a bit scared of social media, scared of what people might think of me. But the reality is, you will always be judged, no matter what you wear, what car you drive, the way you walk or how many pictures of cats you post. So if I'm going to be judged either way, I would much rather be judged having money and being successful.

Listen, if you've got a message which is going to be impactful, if you have got a service like working with investors, then my advice is to get your message out there as best as you possibly can and to hell with anybody who is going to judge you negatively.

Believe it or not, nowadays people call me 'Mr Facebook'! I'm all over the place!

Assets For Life have created our YouTube channel, and thousands of people view our videos everyday. Anyone who watches our videos know they are going to get content and go away with key learning points every time. And just like our networking activities, we are not doing this for the good of our health, we are doing it to get seen and get earning.

At the back end of 2016 I was filming a Facebook live video on location at one of our developments. I started to walk around the site where we were building seven flats and two houses and I had the idea to call the investor who had funded this particular project. I got my phone out to talk to the investor about how things were going.

It was quite a cool idea because it gave fantastic social proof that we can do what we say we can do while also getting the investor to talk live about how ecstatic he was with the way things were going.

A few minutes later I got a message on my phone from this guy called Phil, it just said, "I've been watching you."

I was like, 'Oh my God, I'm being stalked,' and then another text came in from the same bloke. At first I was terrified that things were going to get really weird really quickly but as soon as I actually read the text I was able to take a huge sigh of relief. It read, "I would like to talk about a JV opportunity."

Once I'd taken a couple of calming breaths I called him immediately. It turned out that Phil was based up in Liverpool, was married to a wonderful woman called Karen, had been in property for many years but was looking to emigrate off to Australia so that he and Karen could be closer to their children.

He said, "Look, I love what you guys are doing, we've got access to some cash, we'd like to talk about doing a joint venture." I said, "look, not a problem at all, these things take time, but let's meet up and see where it goes". He lived in Liverpool, I'm living down in Essex, however, I just so happened to be speaking up in Telford the following week so we immediately arranged a meeting there and then.

At the meeting we sat down in the hotel, we got a bite to eat, and I started to listen to Phil; where he was at, what he was doing and what he needs and what he's looking for. He came across as a great guy and he was clearly well informed in the property business. I definitely felt that all-important synergy.

I went on to explain all about what we do at Assets for Life, discussed our product range and how we work. I spoke about Jay and our shared vision, our values and our mission. I also told Phil about some of our other exciting projects that we were currently working on with our investors. Note that never once did I ask him how much money he had. I was there to serve Phil's interests and to try and help him with his situation and achieve what he was looking to achieve.

Once I had said all I had to say Phil looked me square in the eyes and said, "I want to become an investor." I said, "Brilliant. How do you want to get started?" He says, "well, look, I've got access to money, it's not my money, but I've got two investors who are friends of mine and they're sitting on £700,000. Now they trust me and I trust you. Shall we go ahead?"

It was incredible. The first investor put £550,000 into a 12% fixed rate return; the second invested £200,000 on a 10% fixed rate return.

We went into business with Phil and set up a limited company and the investors put their money in using the Assets for Life savings accelerator. That money has been used on one of our commercial conversion developments that we did in Colchester. We've took an office, a B1A, and converted it into 16 boutique 1 bedroom apartments.

That deal would go on to generate somewhere in the region of about £500,000 profit. Of course that's not all of my money, that has to be split four ways; the joint developer, myself, Jay and Phil. But, here's a question for you; how would that change your life, a quarter share of £500,000?

All this from a two minute Facebook live!

So when it comes to social media what you've got to remember is that people are watching. About 80% or 90% of Facebook users are not active, they won't comment or like, but what they will do is watch, and they will watch, and they will watch. And if they are watching you they get to know you, get to like you, and just like Phil, they get to trust you. Trust me, at some point, your watchers will make an approach.

I hope I have managed to illustrate just how valuable it can be to have a solid and current social media presence. At first it can be a bit of an overwhelming task so to make it easier I'd like to share my top tips now on social media marketing.

The most important thing is to go and set up your platforms. I suggest you start with Twitter, Facebook and YouTube.

Have your platforms ready. Start working with one platform on a regular basis to build your confidence and to get your message out there. I recommend you do that using Facebook because it will generally have your biggest reach to the right type of audience. Once you have established yourself on that you can start doing more across your other platforms.

With social media you can get your message out there literally to hundreds of thousands of people very cheaply indeed. You can do a video and post it on your company Facebook page. Alternatively, you can invest £10 a day and produce an advert which could get you literally thousands and thousands of views. You can track who's watching your video, you can then retarget those people. That is just one way in which you can build great rapport and you can get your message out there to huge numbers of prospective investors.

So, ladies and gentlemen, don't miss a trick on social media. Yes, it takes a little bit of time but trust me, it won't take long to get used to it. I hated social media a number of years ago and now I love it! I love getting our message out there to people like you.

That brings us to the end of Step 2. I hope that you've found this part of the portfolio-building process useful. We've spoken about what networking is, how to network, where to network and the power of social media.

I've given you some very clear guidelines and some KPIs to follow, so all you now need to do is prepare, network, get yourself out there, set yourself some targets.

So what I'd like you to do now is to commit to eight weeks' worth of networking. Come on! Get out of your own way and get out there!

Decide what networking groups look good for you and block them out in the diary, get committed – you wont regret it.

This stuff works - Paul Taylor on social media

In 2018 and I found myself living in South Wales. I had decided to pursue my new dream of becoming financially free and generating massive wealth. I had recently seen Liam Ryan from Assets for Life on Facebook talking about developing property with none of his own money and I decided to go and see for myself what it was all about.

In April I attended an Assets for Life seminar in London. In all honestly, I was sceptical as I had never networked before or been to any of these events, however what I learnt on that day opened my eyes to the possibilities and the potential within the property industry.

I then attended the three day bootcamp that taught everyone all about mindset, negotiation, networking, marketing and sales, how to find, structure and finance deals, everything required to get you on your way to becoming financially free one day.

To give you an example of the impact it had on me, even on the first of the three day bootcamp, Liam was giving a talk on the power of social media, and how having a business page was so important and doing Facebook lives etc. to get you and your business out there online. Liam made everyone in the room do a Facebook live, and I asked Liam if he would kindly do one with me to promote my property investment company, Taylors Acquisitions.

Well he did and we did a five minute live on Facebook just talking about how great the day was etc.

Well, within 10 minutes of posting that live video on Facebook, I had a phone call from an old army friend of mine asking me to meet with him as he had 25K for me to invest. I couldn't believe it. After only meeting Liam twice by this point and on the first day of the bootcamp I had raised 25K from a private investor just by taking action and doing what Liam told me to do.

At the same event I met my business partner who just happened to live 15 minutes from me. To cut a long story short, since then we have brought together a solid power team around us, have a pipeline of deals with a potential GDV of over £30m, have purchased an established lettings and estate agency to complement our new build (build to rent) development projects, have a large number of private investors willing to invest seven figures into current projects, we are looking at sites in the central belt of Scotland due to the contacts and new networks we have developed and we have the support and funding availability from local councils to develop in our areas of operations.

We have a 10 year plan to develop our company into one of the leading development and property investment companies in the UK.

Now I'm sure you will agree that we have come a long way over the last few months and without doubt, I would not had made those moves, or realised the potential opportunities that are around us every day, if I hadn't gone to the Assets for Life event and had been mentored by Liam and Jay.

Paul Taylor, managing director, Taylor Acquisitions

Before we go on to step 3 I thought it might be of interest to you to hear from one of our Assets For Life Graduates.

The stories of other's success is a great way to find inspiration particularly as this person knows all about where you are now and where you can be in the not too distant future.

Chapter 13

Case study one: Chris Hopkins

Assets For Life Graduate Chris Hopkins

Chris Hopkins was working 60 hours a week in a highflying corporate job for a big security company. I know, it sounds pretty good at first glance but Chris was unhappy.

He was exchanging time for money, working in a position where he was feeling undervalued. Despite all his hard work and all the time he spent doing it he never quite had enough money at the end of each month. He was feeling frustrated and his personal life had become stale and his professional life had become completely stagnant.

Looking for a change in his fortunes, Chris decided to come along to one our events and immediately signed on to join our academy. Chris was given comprehensive training by Assets For Life in how to build a property portfolio and following our system he raised joint venture finance and has now gone on to do absolutely amazing things.

I caught up with Chris and we recorded an interview so that you can hear from somebody who has achieved what you are about to achieve. You'll gain an understanding of his journey so far, so where he was, where he is now and exactly what he's done to achieve some of his goals. It's an amazing journey; you're going to absolutely love it.

LR: Chris, would it be fair to say that since joining us your life has completely transformed.

CH: Completely. I was struggling to pay my bills working a 60 hours a week in the event industry. It just didn't make any sense. Anyone who has worked in event management can tell you just how much stress is involved in the job.

LR: So, exchanging time for money. I bet you were working more hours than you were being paid for?

CH: Absolutely. I was generally the first one in and the last one to leave. I was working in one of the high profile event stadiums in London. When I was doing the job it could actually be quite exciting, but ultimately I felt trapped, stuck and not really knowing which way to turn. I kept thinking, 'I'm going to be here for the next three or four years. My God, Where am I going to be in five years time?' I was starting to feel deeply frustrated and suddenly knew I had to do something different. The thing was, I always knew wanted to get into property, I always knew it was the way forward for me. It was always something that's excited me.

LR: So what was holding you back?

CH: Probably lack of education and not knowing what to do. I'd never invested in property. I felt I didn't have the know-how, didn't know the right way of doing it. That and I'd only just recently bought my first house so I didn't have the money that I thought I would need.

LR: You're not alone in that Chris, it is mindset that keeps many people blocked from taking action. No time, no money, no experience.

CH: Absolutely but when I saw what you were doing at Assets For Life I just thought, what have I got to lose. So I made the decision to come to the property mastery summit.

LR: And what happened?

CH: I had an incredible realisation, a massive light bulb moment. About halfway through the morning I suddenly realised that, actually, this is achievable! I could do this! True, as I sat there I didn't really have a lot of backing or a lot of support or the time or the energy to actually get out there and do it but it was clear to me that I just needed to change a few little aspects of my day to day life to enable me to go for it. That summit was something I'll always look back on as an incredible experience; it truly changed my thinking and went on to change everything.

LR: So would it be fair to say that attending and committing to coming to the property mastery summit event was a game changer?

CH: More than that, it was a life changer. Getting 1-2-1 time with property experts like yourself was invaluable in taking me forward.

Just being in a room full of like-minded people, all out to achieve the same thing was so affirming of my ambitions. It was a professional and focused environment where everybody was embracing the information that was being fed to us from the stage. With each minute I was there it just became so much clearer that building my own portfolio was a more than achievable goal for me.

I'm a big believer in self-education and bettering myself and going outside of my comfort zone and toward the end of the day, it had been so amazingly helpful in so many ways I thought, 'you know what I need more of this, I want to be part of this' so I committed to investing more of my time into the academy learning experience.

LR: So you came with us for additional training. When you finished the training, and began your journey proper, what was most important to you? Was it cash flow or was it big lumps of cash?

CH: At the start it was cash flow. What we needed to do was to get as much revenue coming in to the business as quickly as possible while committing to as little work as we possibly could. The idea was work less hours for much more money.

LR: What strategy did you decide to start with?

CH: I went to multi-lets. I wanted to get a couple of HMOs in the bag and into the portfolio, high cash flowing assets like that, to create the passive income, in this way I was able to replace my wages quite quickly.

LR: So high cash flowing strategies. Did you have money at the time to implement that strategy?

CH: Nope.

LR: Did that stop you from doing that strategy?

CH: Nope! But I listened and followed the education that was given to me by Assets For Life! I just followed the six steps system step by step and I'm here now today with the outcome.

LR: And you went on to raise joint venture finance?

CH: I did, yeah.

LR: What was your first property deal?

CH: We bought a five bed town house and we converted it into an eight bedroom HMO.

LR: Let me just recap that. So by following our six step system, you've achieved your first property build, no money down. You got your first multi-let, a five bedroom converted to a eight bedroom multi-let in Felixstowe. After all costs, what does that net you per month?

CH: Just a little over £2,000.

LR: Just over £2,000, so from your first deal, that's going to generate £24,000 profit in just year one - that's great. Now I know that £24,000 wasn't enough to replace your income so you are still in your day job.

CH: Yes but Rome wasn't built in a day. I've set a date to leave my employment and focus on property full time and you know how effective setting a goal for yourself is. I already feel so liberated. This journey has taken me pretty much full circle - I've got a business partner and together we have set up our own business. We're buying property into that, and we're looking at bigger and better deals all the time. We've got half a dozen deals lined up at the moment, both looking at HMO high cash flowing portfolio, and also some land developments to build to rent.

LR: So next year's going to be a massive year for you.

CH: 2018, its going to be fantastic.

LR: What would you say to anyone who is in a similar to position to you before you got involved with Assets For Life? Let's say they are in full time employment, no money, no time and sceptical. Suffering from lack of knowledge, and a crippling lack of self-confidence. What advice would you give them?

CH: Believe that change is possible. A lot of people struggle with change because they feel it's going to take them way outside of their comfort zone. And they're right, change can be challenging and sometimes a little scary. But to anyone who's sitting on the fence on this, I urge you to commit. If I can do it, you can do it. If you apply the knowledge, apply the systems and give yourself and set yourself goals, I'm telling you its more than achievable.

When I look back on that interview it fills me with such pride knowing that we have helped someone change their world and achieve such amazing results by following our system.

Chris is just one of literally thousands of people that we've now trained through property through webinars, events, on our boot-camps and of course our academy. And like Chris says if he can do it, you can do it. Right now, you are just one decision, one deal away, from a completely different life.

Step Three

Fact Find

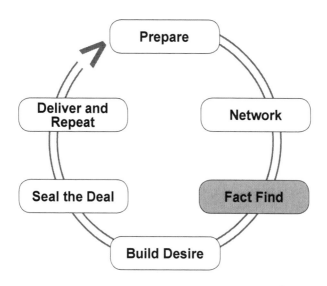

This step is made up of three key components:
The Trust model
Top six questions
Two key JV structures

Chapter 14

The Trust Model

I want you to imagine that you are now in a position where you have put into place everything from steps one and two. Your newly found positive mindset has enabled you to focus on your values and you have a clear mission.

You have a full understanding of how the JV works, a great product range all printed out and ready to give to any would be investor and lastly you have been out networking; collected some cards, booked in a few coffees, and you are now about to embark on your first ever potential investor meeting.

When the time comes for you to go for your first ever coffee the likelihood is that, as the meeting approaches, you will be focused on all the wrong things.

Your fight or flight complex will start to make you feel nervous and it is more than likely that you will worry that it's going to be a complete disaster. You'll forget what to say, you won't be able to answer their questions and the whole meeting will be a total waste of time.

But, here's the thing, if you are not feeling a bit scared and nervous, if you don't have butterflies and sweaty palms, there's probably something wrong with you. This emotional response to a new situation where you cannot predict the outcome of a situation is totally natural and, I might add, absolutely normal.

I remember the first ever joint venture meeting I had (you remember Dave from Basildon) I was absolutely beside myself with nerves. But I had a choice to make; I either do nothing and nothing is going to change, or I do something different to get something different. Now, as you know it went well with Dave and I got him to cross the line with an investment of £5k. However, what I hear time and time again from people who attend our events like The Property Investment Summit is how difficult they find these initial meetings. Having investigated this a little let me give you a few ideas on how to make these first meetings more productive as well as enjoyable!

Ground Rules for your first coffee meeting:

Always remember your potential investor is one of many

Your potential investor is just another human being

Do not put your potential investor on a pedestal

Remember that your potential investor is looking for help

Remember that your potential investor is probably feeling more nervous than you

This is just a cup of coffee and a chat - not the G8 Summit

The meeting should be informative while informal and relaxed

At this early stage we are just going to fact-find and information gather

Your potential investor is not a mark and should be treated with respect at all times

So...

You are not going to do a hard sale

You are not looking to get them to invest every single penny they've got

Please pay close attention to the last three points on the list. The moment somebody feels that you are out to hard sell them or if they feel uncomfortable with the level of investment you are proposing you will lose them. They will go, never to return. Where will they go? They will go to their friends and they will talk about the experience they had with you.

The last thing you need to create is bad word of mouth. What you do need to create is trust and rapport and credibility.

Here's how. I want you to use 'The TRUST Model'. As with a great deal of training/learning models the word trust is an acronym. In this instance it stands for:

T	TERMS
R	RETURNS
U	UNDERSTANDING
S	SECURITY
T	TRUST

Terms

What are the terms of the investment? How does a savings accelerator work? How does a portfolio builder work, or a buy-to-sell type product work? What are the ins and outs of those products? How do you set those products up? What sorts of contracts are in place? Who is responsible for certain tasks? So again, what are the terms of the deal? Who is responsible for certain tasks?

Return

Now, I'm not a financial expert, but from what my clients have told me, some people's ISAs are making them less than 1% per annum. So when you take into account the rate of inflation they're actually losing money!

Any money just sitting in a bank account is a depreciating asset, its going down in value. You can give someone a 6, 8, 10, 12% fixed rate return! You can give someone an investment opportunity where they're going to be making 25, 30% even as high as 50% of the net profit.

The questions your potential investor is most likely to ask is 'how much are they going to make?' And how long are they going to have to wait before they see a return on their capital? It is your job to offer guidance and reassurance on these issues.

Understanding

They need to understand you and you need to understand them.

This comes back to what I was talking to you about in Step One. What is your vision, what are your values, what is your mission?

When a prospective investor gets an idea of where you stand on those things they will have a greater understanding of where you are coming from and what you want to achieve, not just individually but as a partnership. Your prospect needs to gain a proper understanding of the expectations of the joint venture and get an idea of how the relationship is going to work.

It's key to have the correct legal agreements in place so don't do anything just on a handshake. You may use loan/ joint venture/ personal guarantee and shareholder agreements. All of these can be accessed via a good corporate solicitor and people we train well get to use ours.

Security
What security is there in place if any is required? Are you going to put a loan agreement in place? Will you offer a personal guarantee? Are you going to have an RX1 put on an asset? Will the investor have a 1st or 2nd charge on a property? Are they going to become a shareholder in the business?

Trust
People are seeking assurance and reassurance that you know what you are talking about and that you have their best interests at heart. If you have used the T R U and S of the model you will have already gained their trust. And, as you know, when people know, like and trust you they will be far more likely to invest in you.

Understanding and following this trust model is really going to help you when meeting your investors for the first, second or third time. Follow this system, it's going to help you 100%.

As a footnote to the TRUST model I'm about to say something that might surprise you.

If you don't like the person you are talking to or you get a gut feeling that this person is going to be difficult do not proceed any further. Remember, you are embarking on a journey together that will have its ups and down, good times and challenging times and like any relationship, good communication is vital. If you don't like the person you are dealing with it is going to be a long and horrid journey. You need to make sure that you get on with your investor.

Synergy and rapport are fundamental to a creative, profitable relationship.

Chapter 15

Top six questions

Let's put ourselves a little way into the future now.

You are sitting in your first investor meeting and your going through this process of fact-finding and information gathering. While you have the TRUST model as a guide you might still be feeling unsure as to what questions to ask and when to ask them.

Fear not. Based on the innumerous number of investor meetings I have personally had I'm going to give you the top six questions to ask your joint venture partner. You will notice all the elements of the TRUST model coming into play while at the same time, to use an old fashioned sales expression, 'Putting the sizzle on the sausage'.

Always remember, you are not just selling a product but a life choice, a lifestyle and a set of aspirations. Ask these questions in this order and you will start your would-be investor on a journey where the risks are far outweighed by the rewards of what you have to offer.

Question 1:

Tell me what you're looking for in a joint venture partner?

Everybody is looking for something slightly different, so ask the question, what are you looking for. A variant on that is: tell me what you're looking for in a joint venture partner.

Question 2:

Explain to me what you'd like to achieve in the next 1, 3, 5 and 10 years.

A lot of people don't know the answer to this question, or should I say, they have never asked this question of themselves; never considered planning their future because they're stuck in the grind.

Let's face it, life is difficult. Most people are carrying around a big bag of problems on their back and the pressure of their immediate needs stop them from thinking outside the box.

The majority of us are only concerned with paying the next bill, and how we are going to put food on the table. This powerful question will get them to think outside the box and open up their thoughts to get your investors to tap into their vision. With any supplementary questions it is important to get you client to think big, to really indulge their fantasy of what they really want their future to look like. We need to liberate their thinking and allow them space and time to imagine a greater future for themselves.

Question 3:

What does success means to you? Describe what it looks like for me.

If I were to ask that question to 100 people in an audience, I guarantee I'll get 5, 6, 7, 10 different answers because what success means to one person will be different to what it means to me, so you need to find that out what the key motivators are for your investor. This is finding out their 'why'.

Question 4:

What returns would you be looking for?

Take care here. There is no need to be too generous with your rate of return.

I know, 100% over the last couple of years I have given away a 10% fixed rate return and I know 100% they would have been happy with 6 or 7 %, but I went in feet first, I went in a bit like a bull in a china shop, not that I'm really bothered by that because it's about creating a win-win, but what you don't want to do is give away an equity deal and they'd be happy with 6 or 7% fixed rate return.

Question 5:

What does credibility mean to you?

Again, credibility means different things to different people. This question allows you to get an insight into how your investor wants his success to be perceived by others.

And finally, the killer question.

Question 6:

What is most important thing to you in a joint venture?

The answer to this question will give you an idea of how you can offer assurance and security in whatever decisions your would-be investor might make.

These questions show your investor that you value them. The answers they give will help the investor to value themselves and once they have all been asked and answers fully explored your new client will value your relationship. Remember, always come from a place of sincerity, service, and of wanting to help people. It's not about you, it's about them.

Now when do you ask these six questions please don't sit them down and say, "Hey John, I'm now going to ask you six of the top joint venture questions that my mentor, Liam Ryan, told me to ask that will practically guarantee that you make an investment with me."

Don't do that.

The best way of using these questions is to drop them in during your conversation. Remember, at this stage you are not selling anything. You are farming information and data points to sell against later.

Think about this, when you know the answers to these six questions, do you think you can then find the right solution for them? Of course you can! Again, what I love about the stuff I teach is that because I use it all myself I know it works.

I always ask these six questions during my conversation in the first meeting and I always like to keep it nice and relaxed. I'm just saying to the potential investor, "Look, it would be great to know a little bit more about you." It is also the perfect opportunity to find out about their family, their children, their situation. This is information that you're going to need, and again, when you get this information, go and put it in a spreadsheet,

Put it in your CRM system so that you are collecting the data on each and every person that you're having coffee with. Believe me, when you wrack up forty or so coffees over a number of months, it's very easy to forget those people.

I want to finish this chapter by making it crystal clear that these six questions have been instrumental in me raising over £4m in joint venture finance – fact!

I urge you not only to use them but to use them well. They offer you a structure to your initial meeting with any would-be client and they will give you a massive head start in building rapport, harvesting information and guiding your would-be client to take the next step to investing with you.

Chapter 16

Two Key JV Structures

It doesn't matter if you are new to property or you've been in property some time, by reading this book I sincerely hope you are getting excited about the possibilities that will be open to you when you raise joint venture finance.

In this chapter I'm going to be talking about two of the main joint venture structures that we use at Assets for Life. You can use these structures in your business to help you achieve rapid forward movement.

JV Structure One
The Assets for Life Savings Accelerator

We have already discussed this in a previous chapter but I want to get a bit more granular so that you get a more rounded idea of what this JV structure actually is.

The Assets for Life Savings Accelerator is a simple loan agreement, but let me share some numbers around how this product functions to give you an idea of how effective this JV structure is.

So, working through step two of the system, you've been talking to your friends, chatting things through with family members and you've been networking. And now, you're sitting in front of a potential joint venture partner.

Let's assume they have got £100,000 sitting in the bank and you have told them that by letting it just sit in a bank it is a depreciating asset. Their money is worth less and less every day that it stays there. They love the idea of what you're doing and they say, "yeah, you know what, I'm going to invest £100,000 on your savings accelerator product, what type of return would I expect to see?"

For the sake of argument, let's say you offer them 12% fixed rate return, and the time for the contract is one year. Throughout that time you will be in contact with them about once a month to keep them informed and to continue to let them know how thing are going. But finally after the twelve month term of your agreement is up you contact them to say, "Hey John, great news, I'm now in a position to pay you back you're £100,000 plus your 12% fixed rate return, so you've got £112,000, what would you like to do?"

John may say, "Give me my £12,000 and reinvest the £100,00." If John were to do this for five years, at the end of that time you would have made your investor £60,000 on top of the return of their initial £100,000.

That's an incredible 60% return on investment, where else are they going to get a 60% return on investment? They're not - this is why this is very attractive.

But let's just assume the same investor says to you, "You know what? I'm going to invest £100,000, I like the idea of 12% fixed rate return but I'm going to let you compound the interest and you can have the capital for five years." So every year you're going to invest £100,000 plus the interest. Each year the return will grow incrementally from the original £12,000 because you will be reinvesting the original £100,000 plus all the interest accrued thus far throughout the whole five years. This is how compound interest works. At the end of the five years they're now going to make a staggering £76,234 profit, which is a 76.23% return on investment.

Believe me, when you start to put these figures in front of your investors, it's very difficult for them to say no.

Loan agreement examples

This example assumes the partner withdraws their interest each year								
Initial investment	Percentage Return	Return in Year 1	Year 2	Year 3	Year 4	Year 5	Total	Total %
£10,000	8%	£800	£800	£800	£800	£800	£4,000	40%
£50,000	10%	£5,000	£5,000	£5,000	£5,000	£5,000	£25,000	50%
£100,000	12%	£12,000	£12,000	£12,000	£12,000	£12,000	£60,000	60%

This example assumes the partner reinvests their interest each year								
Initial investment	Percentage Return	Return in Year 1	Year 2	Year 3	Year 4	Year 5	Total	Total %
£10,000	8%	£800	£864	£933	£1,008	£1,088	£4,693	46.93%
£50,000	10%	£5,000	£5,500	£6,050	£6,655	£7,321	£30,526	61.05%
£100,000	12%	£12,000	£13,440	£15,053	£16,859	£18,882	£76,234	76.23%

JV Structure Two
The Assets For Life Portfolio Builder

This JV structure is aimed at high net worth and sophisticated investors and by sophisticated I mean individuals who have a good understanding of how investment works.

For these investors we will typically set up a special purpose vehicle limited company in which they will become a 50% shareholder. You will be a director on the business, along with holding the other 50% of the business. Your client will, of course, also be a director in the business. Let us say they invest £250,000 into the company. You will then go and purchase a property, maybe a house that you're going to convert into a multi-let property.

Once you've done the conversion you get the property refinanced through a commercial loan, someone like Shawbrook.

Once again let me refer you to FCA Rules and Regulations 13/3. Check this out and make sure you have a full understanding. We want to keep everything legal and above board.

Shawbrook are a commercial lender, they'll send round the valuer and they will typically value the building based on the rent roll rather than the bricks and mortar value, so you get a much higher valuation. They'll typically then lend 75% loan to value, so you then pull out most of, if not all of, the investment capital, you pay back the investor, and then you own the asset. We do many of our deals with Shawbrook when we refinance.

At this point all of or most OR ALL OF of that initial capital is going to go back to the investor. The property then has a mortgage attached to it and then you own 50% of that asset. On top of that you share 50% of the rental income.

Yes, there is a lot of work to do in the initial stages but look at what you will come out with at the end of it. Half a house and half the rent!

That is the structure explained on paper but how does it work in the real world?

Here's a quick case study.

We purchased a property in Colchester for £151,000. We did an

HMO conversion for a further investment of £53,000 including legal costs making a total outlay for the project £204,000.

We used a mortgage company that gave us 85% LTV so only needed £22,650 for the mortgage deposit and further £53,000 for refurbishment and legals so the initial investment required was £75,650.

The conversion took somewhere in the region of 16 weeks. It is now a six bedroom, four en-suite, high end, boutique multi-let property, renting out to professionals. Each room now rents out at an average of £500 per calendar month. That is a gross rental income of £3,000 per calendar month.

Over a 12-month period, that would generate £36,000 in gross rental income.

Now, with many of our multi-lets, we would either purchase the property for cash, or we get a mortgage at the beginning. When we refinance we will typically do this with Shawbrook using one of our brokers.

Now getting commercial valuations and mortgage is not guaranteed and you need to make sure enough work has been done on the conversion and the house can't easily be turned back into family home. You must talk to your commercial broker to see if there is a good chance of getting a commercial valuation.

On the HMOs that we have had commercial refinanced we have found the following formula is used:

Gross Yearly Rent Income – 20% (Voides And Bad Debt) = Actual Gross Rental Income X 10 = Commercial Value X 75% Ltv = The Amount They Will Lend

So looking at the example above

£36,000 – 20% (£7200) = £28,800 X 10 = £288,000 X 75% = £216,000

We actually ended up being offered a mortgage for £212,000 and from this we paid back the initial mortgage plus investor funds (£204,000) so actually ended up with + £8,000 out of the deal.

This is a no money left in deal for the investor and a no money down deal for us.

We now own half the asset and share half the rental income – FOREVER.

A FREE HOUSE

Now not all deals will you pull out all of the initial investment capital however if through the rental income we can be paid the money left in the deal within three years then we would highly consider the deals.

When talking to your investors don't talk about pulling all the money out, talk about return on capital left in (ROCLI) for example £30,000 left in the deal but the deal makes £10,000 net profit per year that's a 33% ROCLI – where else can your investors find that type of return. Everyone is a winner.

With this particular multi-let property we've got £3,000 per calendar month coming into the bank account. Sounds great but there are a few things that need to come out of that figure at this stage. So, minus the mortgage of £900, bills which is about £80 per room, so roughly £480 and minus some maintenance of about £150 and this particular deal brings in a net profit of £1,470. That's £735 for you and £735 for the investor every single month!

Ask yourself this question right now: how many of these do you need in the portfolio in order to achieve financial freedom? Would just two or three of these deals be enough for you to quit the day job? Would it be enough for you and your family to sleep better at night, for you to start going on that holiday which you haven't been on for the last couple of years?

And when you have done the first one or two of these deals, the next question you have to ask yourself is how many more do you want? How quickly would you like to scale? Maybe you want to do like we did back in 2015/2016 and go large. Can you believe it; we added 11 multi-let properties to our portfolio. And if we can do this stuff, then you can certainly do it as well.

Keep It Legal!

When you are out with your investors and you're looking to structure joint venture deals, it is of paramount importance that you abide to the FCA rules and regulations. The FCA is the Financial Conduct Authority and they offer guidance on who you can and can't do business with ESPVs. Briefly, you need to make sure that you are compliant under the FCA 13/3 ruling. You go against these guidelines at your peril.

To insure that we didn't fall foul of the legal side business we partnered with Optimise Accountants, they are property and tax specialists. Our partnership with Optimise Accountants has guaranteed that we are always covered from a legal stand point. My advice as you start out on building your team around you is to either go to Optimise or look for an equivalent in your area. They will give you all the advice you need to keep you legal and working along the straight and narrow.

In most cases the investor who is putting in the capital for the deal who will be getting a profit share at the end will typically become a shareholder and director on the SPV purchasing the property/site. This person must be a sophisticated investor or high net worth. You as the developer will also be a shareholder and director and by being a director you also have skin in the game as you will be applying for the mortgage/development funding and give a personal guarantee. This gives the investor piece of mind that you have a financial responsibility in the deal.

See diagram (right) of a typical structure with a joint venture partner using the AFL Portfolio Builder.

Funds go from the investor into the joint SPV as a loan. Once we sell or refinance the deal the money goes back to the investor and then we split the profits evenly between the investor, Jay and me.

And suddenly we are at the end of step three!

So, just to summarise, Step 3 is all about fact finding, we have spoken about the TRUST model, we've looked at the top six questions to ask your JV partner, we have also taken a more detailed look at the two main joint venture structures that we use and now we're going to be moving on to Step 4 where you will learn amazing techniques to build desire.

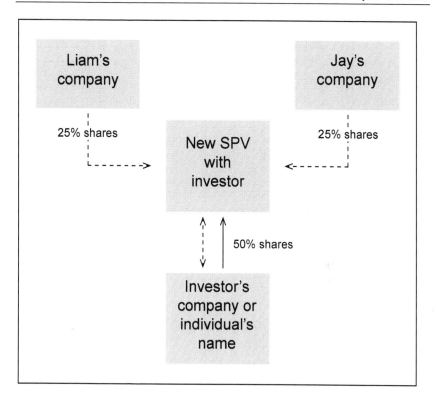

Step Four

Build Desire

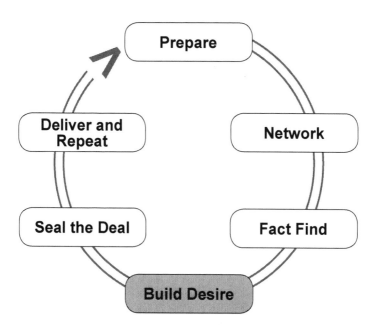

In this step we are going to talk about building desire with your investor/investors. Specifically, you will learn all about:

The power team
How to present the deal
The seven touch point journey to sealing the deal

Chapter 17

Power team

The most important thing to remember when you have your first meeting with an investor is to book in your second meeting there and then.

Whatever you do don't end the meeting with, "oh it's been a great meeting, I'll give you an email or call in the next week or two." Get the second meeting booked in the diary immediately because then that shows commitment from both parties.

On your second meeting you are upping the ante by starting to build desire by getting the investor excited about the opportunities that you have available.

One way in which you're going to build desire, trust and social proof is through your power team. Regardless of what property strategy you decide to use, the overarching model for you, me and everybody is doing less and earning more. I'm a massive believer in leverage.

What is leverage? Basically, getting everyone else to do the work that I'm not very good at and the things that I don't enjoy doing. So what does that mean? What are the benefits to you of leveraging stuff out to other people?

It means that, you're free from all the mundane and stressful tasks that you have no natural ability in doing, you can focus on your KRAs. By that I mean your Key Result Areas. In my opinion, lots of people in the property business, waste their time focusing on the low income generating tasks. Why? Focus on the big stuff, and normally the big stuff in property is finding deals and finding money.

Having said that, I don't really go and find deals within Assets for Life - that is something my business partner Jay does, but then Jay doesn't really go and find the money, that is something that I do. Another example of why you should make sure your business partner has a different but complimentary skill set to you. My time is better spent on social media, doing videos, going out having coffees, networking, building the power team, and making sure that everyone in the team are doing the things that they need to do.

So as you become a business owner, you are going to be the person at the top of the chain, the conductor of the orchestra. You will be the master puppeteer, you are going to be pulling all the strings and when you are in this position you must lead from the front. You need to become the motivator and the one to inspire your team with your vision and your strategy. Most crucially then, at this time, you need to decide who is going to be in your power team when you start building your property business.

You will need:

A broker
You might have a residential broker that can get you your buy-to-let mortgages, or your multi-let mortgages or you might have a commercial broker that can get you your commercial funding for your land development or commercial conversations. Your broker is going to go out and do all the market hunting for you. Based on a strong understanding of your strategy, it is their responsibility to come back with the best deals on the market available at that time.

Agents
You're also going to have an agent of some description in your power team. That might be a commercial agent, a land agent, letting agent or an estate agent. Whichever of those you choose to use you are going to need to build relationships with agents in your desired area that are going to go out there and locate the deals that work for you.

A numbers guy
Once they find you the deals, a certain amount of analysis will be needed. Does this deal stack up? Is it a winner? If you're not great at analysing deals or not great with numbers and spreadsheets then find someone that has a passion and facility with those things. In

Assets For Life Jay Munoz is the man that deals with all that type of stuff. He is our 'numbers guy'. Quiet, passionate and often out of sight from the customers.

He loves a spreadsheet, project management and dealing with the contractors. You'll see Jay from time to time on his bicycle, going round all the streets in our goldmine areas, driving round in his car trying to find the right type of deals. From your point of view find yourself a Jay for your business power team who you can outsource and leverage these types of activity.

Builders and contractors

You're also then going to have builders and main contractors in your power team, these are the people that are going to do the refurbishments and developments. We don't advice that you do the refurbs yourself. The bigger projects the more manpower you will need and so there might come a day when you start reaching out to main contractors for your bigger deals.

Architect and planning consultant

Someone else who is of great benefit in your power team is going to be your architect. They're going to do all the drawings and the plans on various projects for you. They're going to work alongside your planning consultant, because some strategies will require planning or prior approval applications, so again, having a planning consultant in your power team is going to be really important as well.

Solicitor

A solicitor is going to do all your contracts and your legal paperwork for you. You might have a solicitor that is focused on land development or commercial conversions or buying houses. You then may have a solicitor to do all your corporate agreements, shareholders agreements, joint venture agreements with your joint venture partners. And yes your team will continue to grow!

Tax Advisors and accountants

The wonderful thing about becoming a professional property investor and raising joint venture finance is you will start to earn a lot of money. It is vital you set up your structures in the most tax efficient way so you earn more and don't pay more tax than is required. You will need different structures if your trading property or if your buying and holding and also how many JV partners you have. Please get the advice from Optimise Accountants.

Finally, you'll bring in insurance brokers to make sure you and your investor are properly covered.

I know this seems like a long list of people but think about this; if you treat it like a proper bona fide business it will definitely pay you like one. And all of the people I listed just now, they are the ones who will eventually be doing most of the work! Leaving you to do less and you can earn more. Assets for Life are really big on the idea of return on time employed and I'm all about doing multiple deals with multiple JV partners where I don't need to spend that much time on each of those deals, that is where I rely on my power team.

But your power team does much more than just the work.

Your power team will raise your status to almost dizzying heights

When you first start out, one way in which you're going to build desire and confidence with your investor is by talking about your power team. Once you have discussed the JV proposition you can then talk at length about all the amazing professional people you have working for you. By sheer virtue of the fact that you've got all of these highly experienced professionals working for you is going to further install confidence with your investor.

So again, having a great power team is really important in property, using that to your advantage when you're going out and meeting investors is really important. Someone else who should be in your power team is a high level mentor. I also suggest you get yourself into a mastermind programme ASAP.

At Assets for Life we've invested literally tens and tens of thousands of pounds into mentorship programmes, courses, masterminds and audio programmes. Try to understand, you are your greatest asset. And the more you invest in YOU, the bigger return you're going to receive. So get yourself a great mentor and seriously consider joining the Assets for Life academy to further and deepen your education and level of expertise. When you are a part of this amazing group of people, not only will you benefit from our huge network of mentees but you will also build desire and credibility with your joint venture partners because they can see that you take yourself seriously.

This Stuff Works - Kevin D'Souza on Building Desire

There is no doubt in my mind that building a power team helped to create greater desire in my JV partners. I just looked so much more credible. When you can say that you have your own architects, your own engineers, quantity surveyors, interior designers, it really strengthened your status and credibility. People suddenly feel that they are in the hands of an experienced property professional.

In the last 12 months and I've gone from just under a million pound projects to projects that are worth £5.m. I have just closed on a deal that is going to raise me a million pounds in profit. It's unbelievable I know, but it's true. There's no way I could have made that jump without working with these guys, so it's been awesome.

Kevin D'Souza, director, Springboard Property

Chapter 18

Present the deal

Presenting a potential deal to a joint venture partner is very, very exciting indeed. It can also be quite a nerve-racking experience. Let's face it; you might not get the answer that you're looking for. So how do you present a deal to an investor?

By this time you're on your second, third or even fourth meeting with that investor. This could be a lunch or you could be meeting the investor at their house or your house. It could even be out at one of your existing development properties. Whatever the case may be, you're now in a position where you want to put an opportunity in front of the investor.

You're going to know what type of opportunity to present because you would have followed the system and what I've told you to do in steps 1, 2 and 3.

You would have asked the correct questions so you know what that investor wants. It is vital at this stage that you don't come across like a car salesman. And you certainly don't want to come across like you are desperate for the deal. There is no deodorant for desperation so for heaven's sake remember, you've done all the hard work, you've qualified your investor and you are making them an investment opportunity that is right for them. You should allow yourself to feel empowered by this.

Be professional.

Sell without selling

So, how do you do this?

What I'm going to share with you right now has transformed our business and consolidated our hit rate massively. It is a great way to negotiate with an investor and determine if a particular deal is something they are interested in.

Let me explain - when you go to your next joint venture meeting, make sure that you're carrying a folder with a deal that you are going to present or another investor has agreed to commit to. Then your meeting will go something like this.

Here's the scenario:

I've got a meeting now with my potential investor John.

My other investor, Dave, has just agreed to become a joint venture partner. I am carrying the details of this deal with me to the meeting with John.

My meeting with John is going well. We are having a great lunch; the conversation is flowing and relaxed. John is really getting interested with the types of deals that he can get involved with, and that's when I say, "Look John, you're obviously a really smart guy, would you mind doing me a favour. I've got this deal that I have prepared for Dave, another of my clients. Could you possibly have a look over this deal; I'd really appreciate your opinion on it. Is that okay John?"

Of course John is going to say, "Yeah, no problem Liam. I'll be more than happy to have a look over it for you."

Now of course this is a bloody good deal because otherwise Dave wouldn't be doing it, and if you haven't got an investor that's doing a deal then show the investor a deal that you are thinking of doing.

So I go into my bag and pull out a 2 or 3 page PDF document deal. It has a brief but comprehensive description of the deal with a full analysis, the initial investment capital, and a projection on how the deal's going to work and what the exit strategy will be.

I'll hand over the document and say, "Take your time John and give me your views."

Eventually John is probably going to say one of two things:

Probability number 1:

"I'm not interested in this deal Liam, this deal isn't for me," and at that point you would say, "you know what John, that's absolutely brilliant because like I explained, this isn't your deal, this is a deal that Dave is doing and I just wanted to get your feedback. Could you just explain exactly what it is about that deal you do not like."

John is going to go on to say something along the lines of:

"I don't like the area. I'm not really too keen on multi-lets, I'm going to have my money tied up for too long, I'm not really happy with the return on investment."

John is going to give you a number of reasons as to why that deal is not for him and at that point you can say.

"Brilliant, I now have a much better understanding of what it is you are looking for John."

At that point in the conversation, you should say "John, just let's go over it again for further confirmation, what it is you would like."

If this happens you are back to Step 3, fact finding and information gathering. This is all good. You are still in conversation with John and you are showing that you want to absolutely make his deal option as bespoke as possible. Then you can go away and start the process again and arrange your next meeting on the back of the information John has just given you. However, what normally happens is...

Probability number 2:

Having taken a few minutes to look over the file that you have given him John will say, "Wow, this is an amazing deal, can I have it?"

At that point you then say, "I'm afraid not John, this isn't for you, this is for Dave, but yeah, I'm glad that you feel this deal has merit and it's really helpful for me to know a deal like this is the sort of thing that you are looking for too.

"It's got good entry level and it meets exactly with what you want in terms of your time frame.

"From what you are saying you are happy with the level of income that it's going to be producing and as I'm sure you are aware, there's a really good chance of recycling most if not all of the capital. So based on that information John, if I could find you a deal just like this one, is this something you would be happy to proceed with?"

At that point, John is always going to say "yes!"

Now what does that mean?

That means John has agreed to do a joint venture with you but without actually agreeing or shaking your hand or saying yes to a deal.

At that point you're in a very strong position indeed. At this point in the proceedings you then say, "John, you know what, I'm going to go away and I'm going to find exactly this type of deal for you."

What John doesn't know is you've already got another deal like that in your bag ready to present to John at the right point. However, you are not going to present it yet. Building desire is a slow process.

Following this system you are selling without selling. You are taking all of the pressure from the investor and you are getting the investor to give you honest feedback on the types of deals that they would or they wouldn't go for.

Again what John doesn't realise is that you have in fact already presented his deal to him but it's in disguise!

His deal is disguised as someone else's deal. In doing this you have gained John's confirmation that this is the type of deal he would commit to without putting him under any pressure and now John can't wait for your next meeting where you can bring him something to invest in.

Believe me, he'll be ready.

Chapter 19

Seven touchpoints

Getting your first joint venture partner over the line, in most cases, is not something that happens quickly. Building your contact list via coffees and networking meeting will be a gradual process and that is why it's important to have an investor database.

As your contact list grows it's really important to keep in touch with the people you are meeting at networking events so that you stay on their radar and continue to build you relationship with them. Think about it, you have spent time and a bit of money to create these warm leads. Don't let them go cold through neglect. Keep them warm by keeping in touch. But how? What's the best way to do that?

The seven touchpoints
People say is that in order for someone to commit to doing a deal with you, there typically needs to be seven touchpoints along the way before they finally come across.

So let's just go through each of those touchpoints, and I'll explain it to you in a lot more detail.

Touchpoint number 1
Literally the first time that you meet that person. This could be at a networking event, a charity event, it could be someone that you meet in the vegetable aisle at Tesco!

It really doesn't matter where you first meet someone that could be a potential investor, it could be literally anywhere. What does matter is that you come across as plausible and professional. It's important that you're on brand in your image and please always carry your business cards on you. And always be ready to create a great first impression remember everybody will judge you within the first few seconds of you meeting them. So have a great handshake at the ready and always smile when you introduce yourself.

Let's assume you've had a good and constructive conversation and following my system you get your diary out and book in a coffee there and then. So this is touchpoint number 1.

Touchpoint number 2

When you get home send that person an email saying:

"Hi, (person's name). It was a pleasure meeting you earlier. I don't know about you but I definitely a synergy between us. For your interest, I've attached some of our product brochure or our information sheets for you to have a look through. I'm really looking forward to our coffee at Starbucks next Tuesday at 10am. See you then."

Easy!

Touchpoint number 3

This is your first arranged coffee meeting with them. Keep it nice and relaxed. At this touch point we're now into step 3 of the process remember? Fact-finding and information gathering! And what should you do at the end of this meeting? That's right, it is super important to book in the next meeting!

Touchpoint number 4

An email or the phone call within 24 hours of that initial coffee meeting to say how excited you were to have hooked up and what a pleasure it was to see then again.

Touchpoint number 5

Your next face-to-face diary arranged meeting. Start to build your status by choosing a really nice venue for a light lunch. And cover the bill! It shows that you are financially secure and of generous disposition. Treat your would-be client well and they will feel valued. Equally, what better way to get your client to think more highly of you than to take them on a visit to one of your current development sites?

Touchpoint number 6

Another 'good to see you again' phone call or email after your lunch. And finally...

Touchpoint number 7

A business meeting with a heavy social component.

Maybe you'll go and play some golf. Maybe you'll go and have some dinner; maybe you'll introduce them to your family. This is an opportunity to deepen your personal as well as professional relationship.

I would hope by touchpoint 7 that you're in a position where you can then present the opportunity and try and get a yes, and get that investor to commit to doing a joint venture.

The seven touchpoints is an effective structure to work with to build your relationship with a would be investor. However, remember Phil from Liverpool? The first ever time I met him we shook hands on a joint venture, £700,000 but that sort of miracle only happens very rarely. The reason for this is that Phil had been watching me on social medial for a long time so we already had lots of touch points. Most often, we have spent a great deal of time nurturing the relationship that will get people committed to investing money into one of our products. This process has no set timing. It can be a quick as a flash or the process can go over as much as six months.

So you've got to be patient, your perseverance is really important. And remember, consistency plus repetition will always equal success. Yes, you're going to have knock-backs, you're not going to get everyone over the line, but remember, it's only one joint venture at the time, and your next or first joint venture partner could be the one that is going to earn you hundreds of thousands of pounds.

Now, one person within our academy who is doing absolutely brilliantly is Tanner Hicks.

At the time of writing, Tanner has been working with us now for just under a year and his life has been completely transformed. He's done amazing things, for example, in just the last few months he's completed on three multi-let properties, on the back of the joint venture finance he raised! His business has grown exponentially because he understands the importance of putting yourself out there and committing himself to three ideals:

Perseverance

Consistency and

Repetition.

So, lets hear from Tanner.

LR: Tanner, explain where you were at before you came across Assets for Life?

TH: I'd been in property for four years so I had some experience but I wanted to take the next step. I was a busy fool, too much to do, too little time to do it and, at the end of the day, not enough to show for it. When I heard about Assets For Life I just wanted to learn from you and use your experience and guidance to take me forward as a property owner and investor.

LR: So since joining Assets for Life, what are some of your bottom line results you have achieved?

TH: First of all, I think the biggest result for me is actually having more clarity and focus on what I've been setting myself out to achieve. Before I joined you, like I said, I was actually spreading myself way too thin. I was incredibly stressed and as a result I actually burnt out. I had hit rock bottom in terms of what I was trying to do. But with your guidance I've learnt how to restructure what I'm trying to achieve.

As a result I am working much more efficiently. Now I've just completed on three deals, all HMO properties. I have completed the conversion on one of them, another is due to complete next month focus and the last will be finished in due course. My new way of working is get them and set them. It's a clean systematic approach and it keeps me working efficiently but without stress. Before meeting Assets For Life I was trying to do too much, all at once!

LR: So those three properties, what will they net per month?

TH: The first one is £1,400 and that is actually on behalf of a client and the one I'm working on at the moment is going to net about

£1,300 and that's for myself.

LR: This is the power of doing multi-lets, net profit after all costs in the region of 13, 14, 15 hundred pounds per month. How many of them do you need to become financially free?

TH: Literally, any day now!

LR: So what would you say to anyone that is thinking of joining the Assets for Life mentorship programme?

TH: You can see training and being part of mentorships as a big cost and it's easy to think, "Is it going to be worth the value, what am I actually going to get for that?" All I can tell you is that all the training and mentorship that I have received has made all the difference to me.

It took me a while to actually sign up, but you're in a very small community where you build up an amazingly personal relationship with Liam and Jay.

It is still a young mastermind in terms of there aren't loads and loads of people, you don't get lost in a crowd, it's boutique, so you meet people and get to work with them.

I consider Jay and Liam as close friends and mentors of mine now. I can pick up the phone and speak to them whenever I need to. For me that is really important, and I think a lot of people in the group get great value as well.

If you value yourself, invest in yourself. You won't regret it.

LR: What a great note to end on. Thanks Tanner.

Nigel Mansley – on the seven touchpoints

We have been working with Assets For Life for just over a year and already we have a portfolio of nine by to let properties. The key point working in the property business is to get to know your potential partner really well. It may be somebody that you meet through a networking meeting, or through friends and family, but the key thing is to get to know that individual absolutely inside out.

The best way to do this is to work to a plan to help you cultivate your relationship. I recently met a guy at a networking event on the south coast, and we got on really well together and we began to talk about a particular deal. I basically went through the seven touchpoints, so the discussion went over a number of coffee meetings, a couple of dinners, phone calls and emails. After that I really got to figure out whether the investor was right for me. Plus I got a true idea of the availability of the cash on offer and what they want to put in and get out of the deal.

This type of due diligence is vital because personal synergy is key and trust in each other is the foundation of a great forward moving partnership. If there's no trust then things can break down. That can cause a lot of problems and can cost a lot of money later on down the line.

I always follow my due diligence model and it yields great results every time.

Nigel Mansley, Director of Jeris Properties

Step Five

Seal The Deal

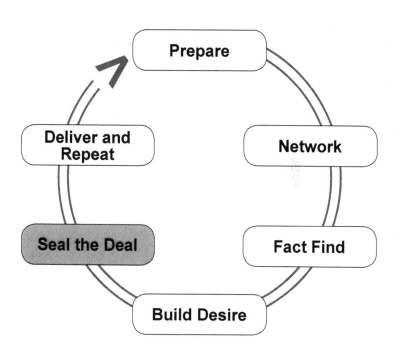

In this step we discuss:
Association
Time to think
The activation agreement
Shaking on it!
Plus...
Case study two: Simon Drage

Chapter 20

Association and time to think

Before we crack on into the main body of this chapter why don't we take some time out right now to take stock of something amazing:
Guess what?
Raising joint venture finance
Starting to live the life of your dreams
More time for yourself
More money
More holiday, bigger holidays, better holidays
Sacking your boss
Creating an amazing business that you can be proud of
Building a legacy for your children
Having a positive impact on the world

All this is possible for you. Right now!

Congratulations on getting to Step 5 of the process. If you have got this far into the book it means you are serious about creating positive change for you and those you love.

Think about this: You are set up and financially free. For once in your life you are actually doing something that you enjoy. You are your own boss and you are having a positive effect on all those around you. How empowering does that sound?

Not only will you grow through this process, so will the people closest to you. But here is a really big question for you- who are those people?

Association
They say you become the average of the five people you hang out with most. Have a think about that for a few seconds. Who do you hang out with most in your life?

Are you hanging out with negative, moaning, skint people, people that are bringing you down? Maybe you are keeping company with people that are not allowing you to be the person you are?

Perhaps the people you spend most of your time with do not have your best interests at heart. Are you living their life rather than your life?

Don't get me wrong, I'm sure your friendship group is full of great people but I'm asking you to carry an awareness of one thing. Broadly speaking people can be characterised as one of two things:

Drains or Radiators

Drains

Drains suck you of your energy and ambition. They replace your positivity with negativity. Often they will pour scorn on your dreams and ambitions. A drain will get you into their bad habits so they are not alone in having them. They moan, they sneer, they belittle and make excuses. Spend time with a drain and you will go away with less energy rather than more.

Radiators

Radiators are full of positive energy. They encourage you to take risks, to go for it. They are happy and successful in their chosen field and they want you to succeed in yours. They are supportive of you but are not afraid to challenge you. Spend time with a radiator and you will go away with more energy rather than less.

Spend a little time to go through the top five people with whom you socialize and decide if they are the right people for you to carry with you as you move forward.

Exercise

Write down now the five people who you hang out with the most – Then ask, are they millionaires? Are they successful? Are they people you really inspire to be like? If you want to become successful hang out with other successful people.

Maybe, as of today, you're going choose to start hanging out exclusively with the winners. With radiators! Think big. When you start hanging out with millionaires and billionaires, guess what, there is a good chance you're going to become one!

When you start choosing to associate with highly motivated active people who take positive action, have a good strong belief system making things happen like we do at Assets for Life, that's going to rub off on you!

This is not just about raising money and building a multimillion-pound property portfolio, this is about you becoming the person you want to be. This is about you becoming happy, living the life of your dreams and working towards your ultimate goals.

Who do you want to take with you? Who is going to hold you back?

Who are your drains? Who are your radiators?

The decision is yours.

Time to think

So, Step 5 of 6 is Seal the Deal. There comes a point when you've been through the process, you've made your seven touchpoints, the proposal has been handed to your possible JV partner, so what do you do now?

Now you have to give your prospective investor time to think. You need to actively take some time out and let them go over your proposal and take in the deal that you have presented to them.

Don't worry if you don't get the commitment straight away. It is a big decision, this investor is going to need maybe a few days, maybe a week, if not longer to digest all of the information before he is ready to make a commitment to invest.

Keep the faith!

Take some time to remember a few key points at this stage.

Thus far you have lead them all the way from having been total strangers to gaining their interest and opening a discussion about JV partnerships.

They have been willing participants in a gentle and subtle process of winning their confidence and broadening their understanding of the incredible offers you can make to them.

Don't get the jitters at the last hurdle and start hassling your investor to commit. That is a sure fire way of making your prospect have second thoughts.

Nobody wants to be pushed. If you push your client you can expect pushback from your client. So don't be scared to back off and by doing that you create even more desire.

Chapter 21

Activation agreement

I'm going to tell you a story that concerns the steep learning curve Jay and I underwent when we were negotiating with one of our first ever joint venture partners at Assets For Life.

We had been putting a great deal of effort into converting a chap from Brighton. He was a really cool guy and he had a genuine and keen interest right from the start. It was all looking very positive. We'd been out on many meetings, a lot of time was invested into the creating the foundations of building that portfolio, and we'd even got as far as setting up an SPV. Jay and I were utterly convinced of this bloke's commitment.

After a lot of scouting around we found just the right deal for him and he seemed really happy with what we had come up with for him. Bingo! It was all set, Jay and I were rubbing our hands with excitement at the thought of this amazing deal coming to fruition. Then, guess what happened?

The day before exchange, the investor pulled out!

He had some issues on his side, he was full of apology and said he felt ashamed after all the time and effort we put into the whole thing but, you know what, these things happen.

We were as compassionate to his situation as possible but all of a sudden we were in real trouble.

Yes, we had made a small cash investment on train fares and coffees and lunches, but the biggest investment was our time.

It was a day before exchange and we were left in a position where we had put over six months into something that just disappeared before our very eyes. Not only that but we'd built up a relationship with the agent and we were left right up the creek without a paddle.

We nearly panicked but I suddenly remembered that we had another investor lined up who might be tempted by the deal we left holding.

After a couple of phone calls and some rather fancy foot work the other investor took the deal. It was a huge relief.

We felt that we had been very lucky in getting it sorted but decided that we never wanted to put ourselves in that position again.

Through this experience we learnt a couple of really important lessons.

One is that you need to get some type of commitment from your potential investor at the very beginning of your negotiations. The way which we do this is through what's called an 'activation agreement', and, it won't come as any surprise when I tell you we haven't done a JV without putting this in place ever since our terrible Brighton shock.

Nowadays, once we're in a position with an investor where they say, "yes, I want to invest, and yes this is the type of deal I'm looking for," bearing in mind we're not deal sourcers, and we may have to go and spend a number of months sourcing the correct deal, what we now do with every investor, we say, "Look, great decision, it's going to be brilliant working with you. What we're now going to do is go in to an activation agreement, would you agree with this? Brilliant."

What is an activation agreement?

Put simply, an activation agreement is a one or two page document that you produce which talks the investor and yourself through how the joint venture is going to work and, as you know, we apply a sourcing fee to the scheme.

Let's just assume this is a multi-let property so the sourcing fee is £5,000. That's a great way in which you can cash flow and cover yourself against loss of time investment if things go wrong at the later stages.

We say to the investor, "to activate our services, you will pay us a £5,000 activation fee, this is to be used as your sourcing fee once we complete on the deal, and as part of you activation, we then have 90 days to go and find you the deal that you have told us you want.

"If in 90 days we do not find you your deal then you can get a full refund on the activation agreement, or you can decide to renew for another 90 days, however if at any point in the process you decide to go and invest in a luxury yacht, or jet, or go on a fancy holiday, or for whatever reason you decide property is not for you, then we will keep your £5,000 for time spent."

When you think about it, that's only fair because there's a lot of tyrekickers out there. There are a lot of people that will say "find me a deal." That's great but we know that finding the right deal that stacks can take some time.

It is only fair that we seek an upfront commitment from the investor before we put that lengthy process into place.

Most people can see the sense in this practice and we very rarely get any kickback on this.

At that point everything is signed off, the activation fee is paid to your bank account, everyone is serious, everyone's committed, and everyone's happy. Plus everyone now knows that we are working on a 90 day time limit to produce a deal that works.

What is that going to do for you as JV partner?

You are going to pull out all of the stops, and we at Assets for Life, have never had to go over our time limit with an investor because we don't want to pay the money back.

We want to make sure we get the deal in place, and since using the activation agreement, we have only dealt with serious, committed investors. If you explain this from the start so the first main meeting so they understand how it works, when you come to seal the deal, which is now step five, there's no hidden surprises.

I advise that you explain all about the activation agreement in your first coffee just so they know how the relationship is going to work out. So, don't make the mistake that we made at the beginning, learn from us, we're sharing this experience with you, ask for an activation fee, get it paid, we use £5,000, you might want to use £1,000 or £2,000 it doesn't really matter, but get some form of commitment.

It covers you, it covers them.
Win, Win!

This Stuff Works - Emma Woodman on The Activation Agreement

I started with AFL in December 2017 with my husband Scott, we started our property business Boscombe Property Group. When I joined my depression and anxiety affected my life severely, I couldn't leave the house or even talk to people I didn't know.

With the help of Liam and Jay I managed to get up and talk to over 250 people about my property journey so far at a property event. I have helped others to see that living with this illness doesn't have to stop you living your life towards financial freedom.

One thing that I took away from learning the No Money Down Blueprint is how important the activation fee is. It is a one page document that outlines what you and the investor want from a deal and over what terms. But the most important thing is that it is an amazing tool that locks in your investor for 90 days for you to find a deal, there is £5,000 non refundable fee which is valid for 90 days. This is used to find a deal but it also makes sure you are only working with serious investors.

I am now meeting many investors and in the process of raising JV finance.

Emma Woodman, director The Boscombe Property Group

Chapter 22

Case study two: Simon Drage

The one thing I can promise you, as a result of following our six step system The No Money Down Blueprint, is that you will find an investor.

Now I don't know what your first investor looks like, it could be someone that's going to loan you £3,000 to help you with a deposit to get a rent-to-rent deal, it could be someone like Phil from Liverpool who invested £700,000 through a couple of investors on a loan agreement, it could be a 50/50 joint venture where you're going to set up an SPV, the one thing I do know is that you're going to find an investor and this is something which I explained to one of our mentees, a guy called Simon Drage.

Simon, when he met us was in a day job, absolutely wanted to get off the tools, had done a little bit of property training before but didn't quite find something that suited him, and he made the decision that he wanted to build a multimillion pound property portfolio, he wanted to use joint venture finance and he started on this process.

It took a little while for him to get over the line, and I know for sure Simon had a few sleepless nights. But patience, definiteness of purpose and sticking to the six step system finally paid off and in a way few of us would have thought possible. Simon's first ever investor has pledged over £1m in joint venture finance, his first ever investor, can you believe that?

Over one million pounds and recently they just exchanged and are now in a process where they are completing on the first of a number of properties working with that million pound investor.

Simon has now completed on three deals and is now looking at using the funds that have been recycled into land and commercial conversion developments.

The wonderful thing about using investor funds is that you can keep using it time and time again from deal to deal.

As of January 2018 Simon has been able to hang up his tools and he is now full time in property. And if he can do it, you can do it.

Who better to tell Simon's story than the man himself.

Simon, over to you.

SD: My company is Willow Bay Properties Ltd and we're a high-end co-living multi-let space company running down in the south west of England. My dad had bought a property and I was working as a builder for him converting it into a HMO. Apart from that I was working 60, 70 hours a week on the tools as a tradesman, no life, no time, struggling on with the daily grind basically, that was my life six days a week. But that was before I joined AFL.

LR: So you wanted something different, but am I right in saying you just didn't quite understand how to go and get it?

SD: Yeah, I'd swallowed up all the free information books on building a property portfolio but I was going round in circles, I didn't know what strategy to choose, and I didn't know where was the best place to go or where to find it.

LR: So why did you join Assets for Life?

SD: I'd been on quite a few property events and every single one just felt like a big sales pitch. They were large sprawling events that were very slick but they didn't have the personal touch. When we came to your day, you explained the process so clearly and gave us your personal assurance that you were going to be there on the end of the phone, the email, Facebook, it really resonated with us. At that point we knew that you were the best people to go with to help us propel our property business in the right direction.

So we joined you, invested in training and finally joined the Assets for Life academy. Over the last seven or eight months it's been absolutely brilliant. We've received expert advice and a great deal of personal guidance.

LR: What strategy did you decide to focus on when you started with us?

SD: Basically I wanted to copy you, so we chose to focus on high-end boutique style HMOs. I call it co-living spaces. And I wanted to acquire the property.

LR: How were you going to own the asset, because from memory you didn't have any money when you came to AFL.

SD: That's right, I had no money and at the beginning I didn't know where we were going to find the money, I just knew it was out there. I just needed to know how to go and get it.

LR: So you were literally starting with no money.

SD: I was in debt, I was minus money!

LR: Can I just summarise the situation you were in when you first came to us. You had no real property experience. Your dad had one property that you were working as a builder. But neither of you had any real experience of how to scale up. At that stage you were working 60 hours a week and could only focus towards building your property portfolio on a part time basis. Plus you were broke. So the only way you were going to achieve your portfolio ambitions was by raising joint venture finance?

SD: 100%, there was no other way that we could build a business or buy properties, own assets, without getting money from some-where else. We knew we had to get a website set up and get our business cards done and then try and put ourselves out there. The best place everyone says to start is property networking events, and business events. We chose to focus our attention soley on the prop-erty events, and just went out there looking to meet investors.

LR: So, you really started to follow our six step system to raise millions in joint venture finance and as a result of doing that I know you started to get results. Can you explain to everyone who your first joint venture partner is and maybe explain how you found them and what they pledged.

SD: I started property networking in Swindon and just started to talk to the investors there. We decided to go to three or four on a regular basis. After a short time we got our faces known and within a very short time found our first investor. He pledged £1 million to buy the properties on a continuous basis so we can keep recycling that cash into more and more properties,

LR: And you're going to use that money to build, buy and ren-ovate a number of multi-let properties, where you will ultimately generate cash flow and own part of that asset.

SD: Yeah that's the plan, constantly going, continuously, we can basically buy three at a time, remortgage number one, buy number four, remortgage number two, buy number five, and just continue on like that. We couldn't have asked for anything better and it all came about from the education and support we received from all the great people at Assets For Life.

LR: I remember when we first sat down with you when you joined the academy we set some goals. As a result of finding that investor, you are seven or eight months into the academy, what has that enabled you to do recently?

SD: As of last week, my 60 hours a week job is now no more. I put the tools down last Friday so I can concentrate on property full time, and get a life back.

LR: I know one of your core values is freedom and spending time with your partner and your great kids, and its only taken you seven or eight months of graft to get to this amazing place.

SD: It's not been easy. We've had our challenges but we had a vision we knew where we wanted to go. As a result of being educated through us AFL and following your system, I've quit the day job and I'm full time in property.

LR: Truly fantastic. What would you say to anyone reading this book who is thinking of getting into property?

SD: The best bit of advice I can give them is to go to your one-day events. Go to the Assets For Life Bootcamp or even joining the Assets For Life academy. You gave me the motivation and the expert advice to get me where I am now. You've got to go out there and find money. Be brave, set up your business, be ready, look professional from the start and then put yourself out there. Use social media, go to networking events and tell everybody you know, and everybody that you meet, what you're doing because you don't know who's got money to invest.

LR: And what would you say to anyone that's thinking of joining the Assets for Life training but might be feeling a bit scared, nervous or sceptical?

SD: Joining Assets for Life is like becoming one of a member of the most amazing family in the world. You just took us in and helped transform everything we did. It's been a demanding seven months but we've got there. The guidance that you've given us has been instrumental in what we're doing now and in how we plan to move forward. You helped us lay the foundations of our business in 2017 and thanks to you guys 2018 is our year.

What an amazing story.
And remember:

If can happen to him, it can happen to you

So that brings us to the end of Step 5 - Seal the Deal. We've spoken about giving the investor space and time to think. I've introduced you to the activation agreement and the importance of having that in place with the investor right from the get go.

You've shaken the hand of your investor and your documents are in place. Now all you've got to do is find the investment for the investor in the next 90 days.

That moves us nicely on to the final step in this very simple six step process.

Step Six

Deliver and Repeat

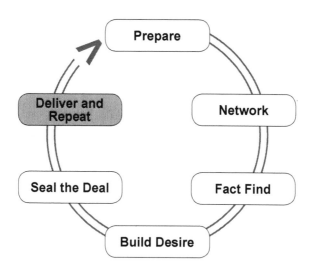

Step six is all about delivering out to the investor and then of course repeating the process, because now you've got your first investor over the line, oh my God, it feels good, and I promise you now you're going to want more, and you're going to want to do more deals and you're going to want to build an even bigger property portfolio.

So onto the final step! In this step we will talk you through three last building blocks to your success.

Deliver and repeat
Communication
Building your reputation

Chapter 23

Communication and building your reputation

You are now in a position where your investor has signed the activation agreement, the activation fee is in your company bank account, and you have 60 to 90 days to go and find the right deal.

Congratulations to you, this is the reality of what is going to be happening when you put yourself out there and you follow this system, you've sealed the deal and you've got your first joint venture partner over the line.

I want to briefly talk about documentation at this point.

It's important that you keep copies of the activation agreement and that you've got passport and utility copies from your investor. It might be that they ask for copies of those things from you too. At this point you can always get your solicitor to deal with this.

This is where the fun really begins because you've now got to go and find a deal, get that deal to stack and get that investor into the deal. Once they come across, of course, there's a whole load of stuff to be doing, from purchasing, to refurbishing the deal to exiting the deal. This is one hell of a journey and you have only just got started.

It is at this point that some people lose the faith and jump ship. Heed the next few words. Take them to heart.

Don't leave the process before the miracle happens.

This will work for anyone as long as you don't give up. It is only a matter of time before you find your first joint venture partner. Remember our second case study Simon? He had ups and downs before he struck gold. But that guy was committed 100% to his education and to his investment. He has grafted and he has kept going; he hasn't given up and look where he is now!

As you've now received the activation fee in your bank and you have started on the 90 days to go and find the investment that they require, I want to discuss the importance of ongoing communication with your investor.

Your investor is going to need to be kept up to date with progress, firstly so that they are up to speed and secondly so that they don't start to get nervous. What I suggest during this point in the process is a phone call/meeting set up every 14 days. This can be a quick 10-minute phone call, just to touch base with the investor so they know what is going on and where you're at. It will help them to how things are going and keep you on your toes too.

Once you find the deal that you want them to invest go and have a nice lunch or a dinner or invite them round to your house and present the deal in a very professional way.

Have your three or four page product brochure on the deal ready to show them, give them the numbers and talk through exactly how the deal is going to work. Let us assume that your investor is going to say, "yes I'm happy to proceed".

At this stage go and set up the relevant companies, or get the relevant agreements in place and share holders agreements depending on how the deal is structured. And once you purchase the property keep having regular meetings with the investor, this is all good for keeping the relationship sweet and your client feeling secure. You may, at some stage even invite them on a site visit.

A great way to keep your client informed on the project is to set up a Dropbox shared folder containing multiple folders and subfolders. This Dropbox link will have every aspect of the deal from analysis to floor plans to mortgage documents to architects planning consultant applications, planning applications. Again this is a highly effective way of keeping up communication with your client, allowing them to see the growth of their project.

When they know they can see anything and everything to do with their deal it gives your client a feeling of personal investment. It is an aspect of our process that we always get great feedback on. At any given point, all relevant information is there for the investor to see anytime they like. This is a great strategy if you're doing a portfolio builder type product or you're doing a buy-to-sell product.

There would be no need for this level of detail if the investor has just loaned you money. In this case you would contact them once a month to touch base and keep the relationship going.

Communication is the key

Don't just get the deal and forget about the investor, because then its very unlikely they will come back and invest with you again. And guess what? Investors know other investors. Treat them well, keep them informed and you're most likely going to start getting referrals and when this happens you're really going to start building some momentum as the relationship develops.

James Fox on Building Relationships

I met Liam in 2015 at a large property event and something about his approach to raising money rang home with me. His approach is simple - do what you say you're going to do, tell the investors about yourself and what you are doing, be open and transparent. He taught me how to engage with lenders and partners; build credibility, trust and secure lending, throughout this he gave me simple tips on working with my investors - keeping them abreast of their investments, how their money was working for them and giving them opportunities to reinvest for future growth.

We secured a deal in late 2017 with the support of Liam and Assets for Life and between our consortium through the steps learnt we were able to secure nearly £2m of other people's money - we helped them secure rates well in excess of bank rates and they have subsequently offered funding for other projects we have been working on.

Since working with Liam I have learnt the power of social media, branding and personal placement in the property sector and have subsequently co-setup a property networking event monthly in the heart of Bishopsgate in the City of London. My life is phenomenally better than just working as a consultant exchanging time for money, I now have choices in when I work and how often I work; I have completed on two projects and am currently running two live projects with three further projects in the pipeline - another tip learnt from Liam 'keep the pipeline full and offers in'.

So total money raised in three years - £7m for deals completed or currently underway plus £5.3m for deal awaiting exchange = £12.3m

Total projects in three years - five projects with 24 units plus one project with 14 units awaiting exchange

Total GDV in three years - £8.6m plus £7.1m for project awaiting exchange

Total profit in three years - £1.9m, £1.526m for project awaiting exchange

The system really does work and I'm so thankful I met Liam and was mentored by him.

James Fox, Littlefox Investments Ltd

Now, one of the great things about getting your first venture partner over the line is that you then have a lot more social proof, you have got history with working with an investor and that is certainly going to help you build your reputation.

So in order to repeat this process with investor 2, 3, 4 and 5, its really important that you deliver exactly what you said you would deliver.

If there are problems along the way don't lie about them. Always be up front and honest with your investors because honesty really is the best policy.

As long as you go with the problem while providing a solution your client will always stay on side.

One of the great things about the property business is that the people within it are very forgiving. People tend to go into it know-

This stuff works - Sacha Bamforth on Deliver and Repeat
I focused my activities on simple loan agreements. My confidence grew after the first deal and went on to deliver and repeat on what was a bit of a no brainer for my investors. They were thrilled with the percentage return they were getting from our

company rather than it sat in the bank making next to nothing or actually loosing value.

We now have five properties, which we were originally going to flip but decided to improve instead. We have been able to repay our investors so all of a sudden we have five free houses!

To add value to the delivery I made sure that I kept the client up to date with how things were going, I paid them back on time and in full and because of this a great number of my investors have just left their money with me on new agreements and are sitting pretty on the rewards. In the meantime I have raised money from investors on loan agreements, and now I own that asset 100%. And I've got 100% of the cash flow, what an amazing deal! Going forward, in ten years time I will have 50 properties in my portfolio.

Sacha Bamforth owner of Let It Be Properties

ing that with any type of purchase there are going to be some bumps along the way.

So build your reputation!

After your first JV projects you can immediately you can get testimonials from your investors. Everything is an opportunity for publicity. You can do some interviews with your clients, suppliers, even members of your power team. You can take photos of you with the investor and post them on social media. It's all going to help with your branding. Other people will be inspired by the investor and what you're doing for them, and, all of a sudden, while that first investor may have taken a few months to come on board, you will find following this system, you will have a queue of people waiting to give you money. And then, like I mentioned at the start of this book, you will have an endless supply of money.

So at this stage of your development:

Communication is important

Building your reputation is important

Doing what you say is important

And,
Your continued education is important.

So keep learning
To keep being the best version of you that you can possibly be, keep reading books, keep listening to audio programmes, invest in property courses, go and invest in the best mentorships that you can possibly get into, like the Assets for Life Academy.

Don't become stale; remember everyday is a school day.

A word of warning!
As your business starts to gain traction and your bank account starts to grow, don't allow yourself to become a big head. When you start making tens of thousands, hundreds of thousands if not millions of pounds in property, remember it makes us no better or no worse than the guy on the park bench.

What it does mean though, is that it does enable us to go and help society and bring value to your local communities. Once you have enjoyed success go and spread the love, do something good because remember:

S + S = S
Serve and Solve equals Success!

So keep serving, keep solving, keep being successful.

Don't get me wrong, it's absolutely OK for you to be successful. Believe me, it is 100% acceptable for you to become a millionaire. If you want fast cars, gold Rolexes, big houses, luxury holidays go for it. But go and raise money for charities, set up homeless shelters, whatever it is you want to do you're just that one joint venture partner, that one deal away from a completely different lifestyle and giving back at the same time.

This is exactly why we love doing joint venture deals, you can do less and you can earn more. Working smarter rather than harder.

I'd rather 50% of something than 100% of nothing, and you just rinse and repeat this process, you can then scale as much as you want to scale.

You might just want to do one of these deals and be done with property for the rest of your life, or, like - Assets for Life you might want to grow a team. We're now a strong team of nine, there's me, Jay, we've got other members in the team working with customer services, sales managers and marketing managers.

We've got the most fantastic and committed people in our team and I wouldn't be here today if it wasn't for them. They keep me to a really high level of accountability; they spur me on and offer emotional support when I need it.

I'm going to keep doing what I absolutely love and nothing is going to stop me because as I continue to use our six step system I can see that our growth is unstoppable. Anything is possible.

Make sure that you follow us on YouTube, Facebook and join the Assets for Life group. Keep your eye out for one of our many flagship events. Please come along and meet us in person. We're a friendly bunch, we love property, we love business, we love working with people like you. Come and listen to our systems and our formulas that you can copy and together we will achieve financial freedom, and ultimately live the life of your dreams. Reach out to us at any point in the future, we're here to help you.

As this book draws to a close I want to leave you with an amazing thought:

IF I CAN DO IT
YOU CAN DO IT TOO!

Printed in Poland
by Amazon Fulfillment
Poland Sp. z o.o., Wrocław

70379049R00092